Take This Job and Thrive

TAKE THIS
JOB
and
Thrive

60 Ways to
Make Life More Rewarding in Today's New Workplace

Anita Bruzzese

IMPACT PUBLICATIONS
Manassas Park, Virginia

Take This Job and Thrive

Library of Congress Cataloging-in-Publication Data

Bruzzese, Anita, 1959-
    Take this job and thrive: 60 ways to make life more rewarding in today's new workplace / Anita Bruzzese.
        p. cm.
    Includes bibliographical references and index.
    ISBN 1-57023-122-2 (alk. paper)
    1. Job satisfaction 2. Career Development. 3. Job stress—Prevention.
4. Work—Psychological aspects. I. Title.
HF5549.5.J63 B772 1999
650.1—dc21   99-41897
                                                                        CIP

Publisher: For information on Impact Publications, including current and forthcoming publications, authors, press kits, bookstore, and submission requirements, visit Impact's Web site: www.impactpublications.com

Publicity/Rights: For information on publicity, author interviews, and subsidiary rights, contact the Public Relations and Marketing Department: Tel. 703/361-7300 or Fax 703/335-9486.

Sales/Distribution: Bookstore sales are handled through Impact's trade distributor: National Book Network, 15200 NBN Way, Blue Ridge Summit, PA 17214, Tel. 1-800-462-6420. All other sales and distribution inquiries should be directed to the publisher: Sales Department, IMPACT PUBLICATIONS, 9104-N Manassas Dr., Manassas Park, VA 20111-5211, Tel. 703/361-7300, Fax 703/335-9486, or E-mail: thrive@impactpublications.com

Book design by Kristina Ackley

Contents

For Len, Nicholas and Ethan
The best part of my life.

And in loving memory of my mother,
Audrey Helen Hess
1926-1999.
A woman of compassion, courage, love, grit and sass.
I did it, Mom.

Acknowledgments

When I first proposed a newspaper column on workplace issues eight years ago, no one was really interested. A female writing about business? About employee benefits and human resource issues? No, thanks, they said.

Until Mike Mika at the *Pensacola News Journal*. He knew I was the former managing editor of *Employee Benefit News*, and he believed workplace topics needed to be covered. Within a few months of the column's launch in the Pensacola paper, Gannett News Service picked it up and began running it nationwide.

The mail immediately began flooding in. From California to New York, readers seemed grateful someone finally recognized the dilemmas they faced every day on the job.

Through their stories and insights I have gained a deeper understanding—and appreciation—for what each person does at work each day.

So my thanks to the readers, the worker bees who sometimes love, sometimes loathe what they do.

But I also want to thank the experts who have offered millions of dollars worth of free workplace advice. They have returned my calls while on the run—sometimes literally racing through airports—to help me make deadlines, and have always been gracious, witty, insightful and intelligent.

And, finally, to the newspaper editors who have run my column. I know that space is a precious commodity, but you've always found some room, and have always been supportive on my efforts.

For all these people, you have made me believe that what I do means something. My thanks.

Anita Bruzzese
May 1999

Take This Job and Thrive

Introduction

When I was growing up, I was raised with all the traditional "girl" skills: I played the piano, took years of dance and art lessons and taught myself needlepoint. I had only sisters, and most of my cousins were girls. We did a lot of girl stuff, like playing dress-up, having tea parties—and as we got older—practicing make-up and hairstyles on each other.

And in our family, my mother and father had a saying: Mom takes care of the inside of the house, and Dad takes care of the outside.

So it came as no surprise, many years later, that I stood staring at my husband's lawnmower, wondering exactly how to turn on the thing. My husband was on a horrendous work schedule, and the lawn needed cutting. The answer was simple. I would cut the grass.

I circled the thing in my driveway, thinking: "How hard can it be?"

Fortunately, there was a little picture of a man starting the machine already on the mower, so I managed that part of it okay. Then, envisioning my father's and my husband's mowing ventures in my mind, I started out.

Did I mention it was the middle of summer in Florida? And although it was early morning, the day was so humid I felt as if someone was holding a wet towel over my face?

"I've given birth," I kept telling myself. "Twenty hours of labor. How hard can this be?"

About 10 minutes into the process, the sweat was pouring off my face, and my heart was beginning to pound. The yard had a slight rise, and 15 minutes later, it felt like I was trying to mow up Mt. Everest. By this time, the man next door had started to mow, waving jauntily when we passed near each other. He didn't seem nearly as winded, and I was beginning to flag terribly.

Thirty minutes into the work, my heart was pounding so hard I thought that it was going to leap out of my chest. "Can you have a heart attack at 30?" I wondered. My body was nearly horizontal—my arms locked straight in front of me and my legs digging in behind me as I attempted to push what seemed like a 500-pound mower the last few yards.

Finally, it was over. I dragged the mower to the side of the house, never even considering doing the back yard. It was fenced. No one could see it.

After my heart rate slowed, I showered, guzzled liquids and collapsed on the couch to call my husband at work and tell him of my feat.

"You know," I said to him. "That is such a hard job! I don't know how you do it every week! I am absolutely amazed!"

"Yeah," he agreed. "Just think of how hard it would be if the mower wasn't self-propelled."

"Self-propelled?" I questioned, my voice a bit weak. "What's that?"

"You know," he says. "You push down that lever on the handle, and the mower just kind of takes off by itself."

"You're kidding, right?"

He started to laugh, and quickly stopped when he heard the heavy breathing coming from my end.

"No. Oh, no. You didn't push that thing all by yourself, did you?"

"Yes. I did," I said, my teeth clenched together, perhaps permanently.

Needless to say, a week later, I approached the mower with a whole new attitude. One of confidence, born through new knowledge and new understanding. I not only mowed the front, I mowed the back and waved jauntily to the neighbor getting his newspaper across the street.

After showering, I called my husband at work.

"By the way," I said. "That isn't so hard. And you're not that amazing after all."

I hung up, the sound of his laughter in my ear.

The reason I tell this story (besides the fact that all my male relatives love to hear it), is that in the workplace today, we often suffer because of our own ignorance. And many times, just as in my case, it's not something we consciously do, we just don't think to ask the right questions, or get the right information.

As a journalist for nearly 20 years, my training has taught me to ask questions and to accept nothing at face value. And yet, that lawnmower made me forget all my training. I felt like I was missing something, but I couldn't think of what it was. So, I just figured this was a job I couldn't do, or at least couldn't do nearly as well as my husband.

But I made several big mistakes: 1) I didn't do my home-work, 2) I didn't ask questions, 3) I didn't ask for help and 4) I didn't stop to evaluate the situation even when I knew deep down there was something wrong.

And that's often what happens in careers and in the workplace. We get so caught up in the task at hand and the stresses of the moment, that we forget to step back and assess where we are. Somehow we think there is something wrong with us because we haven't achieved the success that others have, or attained the future we envisioned for ourselves.

In the last six years, I have talked to dozens of workplace experts for my nationally syndicated newspaper column for Gannett News Service called "On the Job." I've also received hundreds of letters from readers all over the world asking for advice, or simply relating their experiences at work. What I have learned is this: there is no "Holy Grail" of career strategies. Sometimes experts don't agree on the best strategy, sometimes what they recommend simply won't work in certain workplaces. But I do think that knowledge is power, and informed decisions are the best ones.

As a journalist, I get the facts, and try and balance the information fairly and report it accurately. I wrote this book with the knowledge that no two work situations are the same and no individual should be forced into a mold. But the information in this book is designed to get you thinking, and possibly on the road to action.

There is no reason you cannot be self-propelled. And then, I think you truly will amaze yourself.

1

PERSONAL IMPROVEMENT

My first summer job was at 14, washing out communion cups for a local church. In this particular parish, grape juice—not wine—was used and distributed to the faithful in little cups that looked like oversized thimbles. My job was to gather the cups in buckets on Monday morning, and wash them in a solution of bleach and water so they could be used the next Sunday.

Problem was, no one really explained (or at least never explained it enough to my mind) exactly what the breakdown of that solution should be. So, armed with the knowledge that at home my mom added at least a cup of bleach to every load of laundry, I did the same. For every bucket, in went at least a cup of bleach.

After a while, the little room in which I worked started to fill up with some pretty nasty fumes. Between the strong smell of bleach, old grape juice and the piece of cherry pie I had for breakfast, my stomach and head were trying to switch places.

Fortunately, about the time I started seeing the world in a sort of pink haze, the janitor arrived to check on my progress.

After yanking me outside and getting me a cold soda from the church's vending machine, he explained that only a drop or two of bleach should be added to each bucket of water. For his advice, I was eternally grateful—and I'm sure the unknowing parishioners would have prayed for his good health every day if they knew they had been saved from sipping grape juice from cups saturated in bleach.

I remember at the time thinking that although I appreciated his advice, I wasn't overly concerned with the process. I didn't plan on sticking around past August, after all, and I sure as heck wasn't going to be returning next year because I planned on landing a more promising position.

Even at 14, I knew my first job wouldn't be my last. And that's how it is in the labor market today.

No one expects to be with a company 30 years any more, getting the gold watch and retiring to a cabin on the lake. Experts say most people will average about six different jobs in a career lifetime, and some of that will not be by choice.

More companies treat employees as commodities that can be bought and sold, depending on shareholder demands and bottom-line expectations. And while younger workers are more likely to job hop by choice—and have no trouble landing positions because of highly sought-after skills such as computer knowledge—other workers must confront bigger concerns.

Faced with mortgage payments, car loans, braces for the kids and trying to save for the future means that workers need to get the best job they can, and constantly improve and hone their skills. So this chapter offers advice on how you can make yourself a hot commodity—not an expendable one.

———◆———

The Inside Skinny on Those High Achievers

You've put your nose to the grindstone, you get your work done on time and you are never late. So why is it that others seem to be enjoying more success than you?

Unfortunately, in today's workplace, there are many things at play beyond a good job performance. There are more subtle issues involved that may determine whether your career takes flight, or takes a beating.

Michael Mercer, an industrial psychologist, has made it his business to find out what makes some people shine, while others fail to thrive. He says that his research has found that people who advance quickly in their careers:[1]

1. Make a great impression on nearly everyone they meet.
2. Can smoothly negotiate, influence and persuade others.
3. Strut their stuff and act like high achievers.
4. Lead highly productive meetings.
5. Give super presentations.
6. Write clear, crisp, concise memos, reports and letters.

So now that you have an idea of what impresses the boss and others, how do you go about doing it? Mercer (who actually followed these people around) says that he found there are some pretty clear-cut strategies to use if you want to become one of the high achievers.

Begin, he says, by looking around you. Are you part of the group, or do you stand apart? Sure, everyone is unique, but the fact is that people want to be around others who are like them. That means if the boss is detail-oriented, then you need to learn to focus on details. If your manager is more happy-go-lucky, have a joke ready, or a fun idea to let off a little office pressure.

In addition, try to match your body language to that of the person you are trying to impress. If the person is soft-spoken, modulate your speech. If the person uses a lot of hand gestures, then become more animated. The point is to try and make the person feel more comfortable with you—because you are not so different from them. Get it?

Along these same lines, Mercer suggests you:

- ☑ **Use the "pace-and-then-lead" technique** to make people feel comfortable when you are trying to negotiate with them. This means that you agree with them on some point, which helps them relax. Then, you can more easily lead them in the direction you want them to go.
- ☑ **Have a "can-do" attitude.** Try to be positive and upbeat, and avoid using the word "try."
- ☑ **Keep the meeting rolling.** Start on time, have an agenda, end it on time.
- ☑ **Be prepared.** When giving a presentation, have visual aids, speak at least 50 percent to 100 percent more loudly than you do normally and be enthusiastic about your subject.
- ☑ **Write well.** High achievers tend to use more active, rather than passive, verbs and use subheadings and subtitles with shorter paragraphs.

But just how important are these skills?

"Being competent in your work plus 50 cents will get you a cup of coffee," Mercer says. "Being competent in your work plus making a fantastic impression on the people who count will get you a minimum of $75,000."

Is That a Light Bulb Over Your Head?

You've got a great idea—you're fairly bursting with the news that this brilliant concept will not only save the company time, but money as well.

But wait a minute. Who are you going to tell? *Are* you going to tell? Maybe you're worried the idea will sink like the *Titanic* once management begins to pick it apart, so you decide to keep it to yourself. But you start to feel bitter about it, and then after a while, you start cursing management and the company under your breath. You're dead in the water at the company, you think, might as well move on.

No, wait!

It could be that you simply don't know how to persuade those in charge to listen to you. There is, however, a way to become more persuasive in your work life—and the greatest benefit is that this skill can benefit your personal life as well.

Norbert Aubuchon is an expert at persuasion. He conducts numerous seminars and tells participants that building a better mousetrap is not a guarantee of career success. Rather, it's finding out what others need and then giving it to them that will move you up the ladder.

"People do not understand that persuasion is a process," Aubuchon says. "It's an unforced force that can move the world."

Aubuchon explains that unlike negotiating with others or commanding them, persuasion is the one form of communication that is non-adversarial—and people usually end up feeling comfortable and satisfied with the results. No one really likes being commanded, and negotiation usually involves giving up something to satisfy someone else, he says.

"What's more powerful than getting people to do what you want them to do and having them like it?" he says.

Aubuchon stresses that just because you are smart, hardworking and have innovative ideas doesn't mean others will automatically listen to you. So how do you get your idea through the tough decision-making process at your company? He offers these tips:[2]

- ☑ **Ask questions.** Find out what is needed in the company. It's amazing what you will hear once you keep your ears open. Then tailor any project to answer those needs. Quiz your boss about company needs, attend events that put you in a position to query other top brass.

- ☑ **Do your homework.** The task should be important and timely, one that can be acted on soon. Develop costs, time, number of people required, quality, quantity, earnings, payback, etc. Know your subject inside and out—be able to answer who, what, when, where, why and how.

- ☑ **Define your objective in 50 words or less.** State exactly what you want to accomplish as a result of the proposal.

☑ **Be flexible.** You will have to tailor each phase of your project to meet individual needs as it moves through management. Make sure you follow the rules of hierarchy. No jumping over your boss to get to the person higher up. As you gain success with each step, make sure you reassess the needs of each person.

☑ **Don't fall in love with your project.** That's a recipe for disaster because it keeps you from thinking objectively and prevents you from thinking of the other person's needs.

☑ **Practice, practice, practice.** Persuasion is not an easy task, and it might take several tries before you are successful. If the project fails, it probably is because you missed a need, or perhaps you were handed some false information. Just keep in mind that each attempt refines your process and makes you smarter and better at achieving your goal.

"This structure is no panacea, but it's the way to go in today's workplace," Aubuchon says. "We need all the good ideas we can get."

Yoo Hoo! Over Here!

You've kept your nose to the grindstone, working long hours, dedicating yourself to the company and to your job. So how come when promotions were passed out, you were passed over?

Stephanie Sherman, a management and workplace expert, says that the biggest mistake people make is not having a strategy for getting noticed on the job. She quickly adds that being memorable does not mean calling attention to yourself by acting like an idiot or being a pest, but rather by developing an image that enhances your natural abilities.

Here are some tips:[3]

☑ **Get involved** in high-visibility projects. If it costs a lot of money, has a high impact on a lot of people or is considered high risk (like launching a new product), get on board.

☑ **Be on the team.** Teams offer you a good chance to broaden your skills and knowledge, and help you get to know other people in your company, while giving others a chance to work with you.

☑ **Become active** in "select" social and community opportunities. Find out what activities your company sponsors and attend them as well as company social functions. Be on your best behavior; you don't want to be memorable for the drunken conga line you led on the head table.

☑ **Align your energy and your initiatives with those of the company.** Create opportunities for yourself with your suggestions. "Don't be afraid of rejection," Sherman says. "Just because they don't accept your idea doesn't mean it was not any good, but perhaps it wasn't the right time for it, perhaps because of the money."

☑ **Take the job no one else wants.** It may be a pain-in-the-neck task like dealing with a difficult customer or organizing an inefficient operation or relieving the boss of a detested job. But you then become the person recognized for putting a positive spin on tough issues. Or, become the one who can quickly find the answer to a question, making you a resource "guru."

☑ **Be the cheerleader.** Nominate your boss or your team or your organization for awards. By making them look good, you look good.

Still, even by following all these suggestions it may not be smooth sailing. Sherman notes that "bungee bosses"—those managers who come and go with alarming regularity—can make it tough to maintain your own popularity. In this case, Sherman says it's best to go slow until you get a full understanding of what the new boss likes and dislikes before jumping in with new ideas.

"Slower is better so that you don't get the reputation with them of being a brown-noser," she says.

And, with more managers traveling, it may be tough to make sure your efforts are recognized from an airplane 30,000 feet over Cleveland. Sherman advises that you must keep in communication with managers on the go, sending them company newsletters, or articles that appear relating to the company or your industry.

At the same time, you've got to be careful that you don't make co-workers resentful of your behavior. Sherman suggests inviting co-workers to participate with you on projects or attend activities with you. She also advises giving others praise and compliments "to be supportive of them and what they do."

And remember that modesty is the best policy.

Charming the Birds Out of Trees

We've all met that person on the job who has that special something. It's hard to put your finger on it, but the best term you come up with is "charisma."

And while that term has been used to describe everything from preachers to punk rock stars, charisma is actually something each of us has—and what the most successful people learn to develop and use to their advantage, says Tony Alessandra, a motivational expert.

Alessandra defines charisma as "the ability to influence others positively by connecting with them physically, emotionally and intellectually." In other words, it is what makes other people like you and want to follow you, even if they don't know much about you.

He says that while we have the "seeds of charisma" within us, we may have personality traits that are stronger in some areas than others. The key, he says, is developing those other areas so that our full personality is developed and our charisma comes shining through at work.

"Some people may feel charisma is not a good thing, that it's phony. It's true some people can fake it, but that's short-term charisma. Sustained, real charisma is magnetic. It truly draws people to you. It makes you stand out," Alessandra says.

And in today's workplace where skills must constantly be upgraded, and changing jobs is inevitable, Alessandra says he believes that "charisma transfers across the board."

"Everybody can benefit from developing their charisma," he says. "Charisma makes people want to do things for you because of their relationship to you."

Alessandra describes the main components of charisma as:[4]

1. **The silent message.** Do you look people in the eye, or stare at your shoes when talking to them? Do you walk into a room confidently, shoulders back? Or do you shuffle in the door, then hug the wall? You are silently shaping your personal message with your body language—the way you look, the way you walk, the way you shake hands.

2. **An ability to speak well.** No one will hear your terrific idea if you cannot articulate it.

3. **Listening.** "People do not realize how much power there is in listening," he says. He adds that it is a skill that can be improved easily, and is a key to communicating and making others feel special in your presence.

4. **Persuasion.** What abilities do you use to motivate others to follow your lead or persuade them to your point of view? Your idea may be terrific, but what good is that if you can't sell it?

5. **Valuing personal space.** There's a time to get close, and there's a time to back off. The key is knowing which one will make a person feel at ease, then doing it. The same is true for time— you must be respectful of scheduling conflicts faced by other people, but also recognize others may need more of your time.

6. **Adaptability.** Do you listen to views you don't agree with on a call-in radio show, or do you turn the channel in disgust? Your ability to listen to others, to be nonjudgmental and to be open to new experiences translates itself into building bridges with people of other cultures, generations and backgrounds.

7. **Envisioning victory.** You must have a passion for your ideas, for your ability to create and sustain change that will truly make a difference. You must care deeply for your objective.

Alessandra points out that no one will become charismatic overnight, especially since some people become paralyzed at the thought of failure or change.

"Look to improve yourself a little bit at a time," he says. "Have a true desire for self-improvement, and it will happen."

If you're interested in your "charisma quotient," visit Alessandra's web site (www.alessandra.com) where you can take a quiz that will ask you questions and then direct you to a self-help guide based on your score.

Save the Hissy-Fits for Friends

The workplace today can be highly emotional. We spend more hours than ever before on the job and we are required to perform at peak levels while doing the work of two or more people. On top of that, we really would like to give the arrogant manager a good kick in the hard drive and boot the whiny co-worker out the door.

Is it any wonder that resentment or anger or feelings of helplessness reach such a level one day that the dam bursts? For some, this may mean tears, or for others, it may erupt in anger or a quick jab to an unsuspecting vending machine.

Whatever the reaction, we may quickly become embarrassed by our emotional outburst, followed by feelings of dread as we notice the reaction of a manager or co-worker. They may look away, they may ignore us, they may look at us with pity.

William Lundin, a psychologist and workplace trainer, says it can be dangerous to express emotions to managers who don't know how to react to such displays. A job, he says, can actually be threatened by emotional displays that make others feel so uncomfortable they don't want to deal with you.

Of course, in a perfect world, a little emotion would be considered healthy for clearing the air and putting things into perspective while resolving conflicts. But that's not the way it works in the workplace.

"Unless the company helps you express yourself and encourages you to do so, then you must find a substitute arena for your emotions," Lundin says. "We are cautioning people to be very careful about emotional outbursts in the workplace."

Instead, he says you should take your problems home to a loved one, confiding your pain to a trusted person who will accept your feelings.

"This has the added benefit of enhancing your personal relationship," Lundin says, "while helping you stay cool at work."

Other advice:

☑ **Role play.** Get a friend or spouse to help you practice how to handle situations that make you emotional. By preparing yourself, you feel more confident and take some of the volatility out of the situation.

☑ **Discover your flash points.** We all have those issues that get under our skin. Look closely at where you are vulnerable and see how you can better cope—either by avoiding explosive situations or by finding positive ways to deal with your anger.

☑ **Learn to keep your mouth shut.** There are bosses who like to blind-side you with anger that leaves you reeling. The unwarranted attack by such a manager may prompt a very emotional response from you—shaking hands, blood pumping to your face, sweat breaking out all over your body—but don't let on that you have been affected.

"Don't have a hair-trigger reaction, and don't blow up," he says. "Just listen and then get away as soon as possible to deal with your emotions in private. And remember, not everything that happens at work is your fault. When things get tough, remind yourself what you're worth as a person."

☑ **Step back.** When you find yourself becoming overly emotional about work, it's time to step back. Get involved with a hobby, sport or other activity that takes your body and mind away from the job. Consider keeping a journal to write down your feelings.

Using the Right Soup Spoon, and Other
Critical Business Issues

If you were the kind of kid who ignored your mom when she was nagging at you to get your elbows off the table and sit up straight, then you blew it. Because when mom was constantly reminding you to say "please" and "thank you" and to wipe your mouth on a napkin and not on your sleeve, she obviously had your future business success in mind.

"Good manners can save careers or start some careers," says Hilka Klinkenberg, an etiquette expert. "Some companies purposely preorder difficult foods at a lunch interview to see how you handle it. And while you may think that if you get taken out to lunch that you are going to get the job, think again. They're going to be watching your manners and see if you let the conversational ball drop."

Surely, you think, slurping your soup or slumping in your seat won't hurt your chances of getting a job. But think of it this way: if your bad manners and sloppy habits distract from a presentation for an important client, it may cost you a deal, a promotion—and a job.

"I had one client who asked me to work with this young executive who was very sharp, but he refused to work with me on his manners," Klinkenberg says. "Eventually, he had to leave the company."

Klinkenberg says if you are interested in improving your manners, the first rule is to remember that business etiquette is not the same as social etiquette.

For one thing, a male employee who is overly polite to female employees may be accused of sexual harassment. At the same time, women must accept common courtesies from men without feeling harassment is taking place. By opening a door for a woman juggling a heavy box, a man is simply being polite and the woman would most likely do the same for him.

Here's a good rule of thumb: how you treat someone in a business environment should be based on the hierarchy and position you hold. If you're the boss, you don't run and hold the door for every person who crosses your path. If you're an employee, hold the door for the boss— especially if this person is loaded down with paperwork. Keep in mind that gender has no basis.

And while bad manners can kill a deal or hurt a relationship with a boss, they also can damage relationships among co-workers. Yelling across an office, snooping around someone else's desk and bypassing people with memos are all impolite behaviors. Saying "please" and "thank you" and "good morning" can go a long way toward instilling good will among peers.

That's not the way business is done, you say? Snooping is just being business savvy? Being rude and aggressive is what gets you up the corporate ladder?

"When you are doing any of these things to garner prestige for yourself, people know what you're trying to do, and it just looks petty," Klinkenberg says.

Klinkenberg adds that just as good manners must be taught to children by their parents, top executives must set the example for employees. If not, impolite employees may run off customers, and make working with peers a miserable experience.

So, listen to mom. Sit up straight. Get your elbows off the table. And remember to say "thank you" when you get your next promotion.

Hang Up on Bad Telephone Habits

How do you answer your phone at work? Do you rattle off your name so fast that the person has to wonder what language you are speaking? Do you grunt responses like you just got socked in the gut with a bowling ball? Do you hang up before the other person finishes saying "good-bye?"

If this sounds familiar, you need help. Your telephone habits are sick, sick, sick, and they're making other people mad, mad, mad.

Nancy Friedman should know. She hears loads of complaints from people fed up with bad telephone behavior. In fact, the problem is so bad that she's founded an international business and become known as "The Telephone Doctor," in St. Louis, Mo.

"We graduate people with (college) degrees up their arm, but they're rude to people on the phone," Friedman says. "I teach a lot of plain old common sense."

Friedman says the problem is that people are not friendly enough.

"Callers should be treated as a welcome guest," she says. "You can be fun and happy and businesslike. Being nice doesn't mean you're not being professional."

Friedman says that the first four to six seconds of a call are crucial because that's how long you have to make a good first impression. She advises that each time you answer the phone, begin with a buffer, such as "Good morning." If the phone has rung more than three times, begin with "I'm sorry it rang so long."

Next, confidently and clearly state your company or department name, followed by your name. Scrap the standard, "Can I take a message?" Instead, try something like "Ms. Park is in a meeting until 2 p.m. This is Fred. I'm her assistant. How can I help you?"

Remember that usually there are several people who might be able to help a customer or, at least get the ball rolling. If someone is calling your company for the first time, it doesn't matter to them who answers the phone, because the person answering the phone is that company—whether it's the CEO or the receptionist.

If you aren't friendly and helpful to a customer, Friedman says, "you'll lose business and you'll lose revenue. Your image is as important as the bottom line."

And, as a final lesson, Friedman says there are five forbidden phrases that you should strike from your telephone conversation when dealing with a customer on the phone:

- ☑ **"I don't know."** If you don't, find out.
- ☑ **"I can't do that."** Say what you can do and try to find an acceptable alternative. If you just cannot work it out, admit that you tried but that it is difficult. Ask for suggestions from the other person.
- ☑ **"You'll have to."** The only thing the caller has to do is get peeved at hearing this. Use phrases like "you'll need to" and "here's how I can help you with that."
- ☑ **"Hang on a second, I'll be right back."** Unless you're Superman, it's going to take you longer than that. Tell the caller it will

take a few minutes and ask if they want to hold. Most people will be patient longer if they have a time frame.

☑ **"No."** Never begin a sentence with it, and avoid it when possible. Try instead: "I cannot refund your money, but I can replace the product at no charge."

Speaking of Success...

You've been called on to make a speech. Do you look forward to it or would you rather submit to some physical torture that entails breaking body parts? If it's the latter, you're not alone. Many people are intimidated, stressed out and scared spitless at the thought of getting up in front of a bunch of people and speaking.

And yet, as your career grows, so probably will the number of requests to give a speech. Your expertise in a given area is desired, so you should be flattered. So then why do feel like throwing up?

First, take a deep breath. Now, listen to some expert advice on how to give an effective speech. And hold onto this thought: it does get easier with time.

"I think the most common mistake that people make is going on too long when making a speech,' says Cy Charney, a national speaker and author of books on training and the workplace.

Other common goofs, according to Charney, include giving anecdotes that have nothing to do with the subject or the audience, or the inability to stop apologizing for nervousness.[5]

"When you talk about problems—like your nervousness or materials you forgot—then it makes the audience focus on the problem and wonder if you're going to make it through this or not," he says.

If this sounds like something that has happened to you, don't despair. There are key ingredients to a good speech, and Charney concedes a little nervousness is beneficial, because it gets the blood pumping and keeps the enthusiasm high.

First, you need to do a little research. Consider the audience—the age, gender, background and education. Next, establish an objective—something you will use to drive your point home toward the end of the speech. After drawing a mental map of what you want to get across to your audience, develop an outline of key points with a natural flow of ideas.

Use 3 x 5-inch cue cards as reminders or prompts for each key point, but don't write out your speech. There's nothing more boring to an audience than listening to someone read a speech, which sends your voice into a monotone that could cure the worst of insomniacs. Speak to your audience as if the members were sitting in your living room, smile at them and make eye contact.

"Look out into the audience and find that friendly face that is nodding and smiling at you, and look to them for reassurance when you need it," Charney says. "Try to avoid the person sitting there with arms crossed, not smiling. That will only add to your nervousness."

More of Charney's advice:

☑ **Use personal anecdotes** to make your audience feel comfortable. One of Charney's favorite stories on conflict resolution has to do with his wife effectively stopping a very large man from sticking his dirty hands into a store's salad bar, asserting herself in such a way that they man halted his behavior and backed away.

☑ **Challenge your audience** by starting off with who, what, when, where, why and how questions. Or, quote a shocking statistic or take a controversial stance.

☑ **Use humor only if you won't offend** anyone or if you're good at telling jokes. The best humor is a story that is self-deprecating.

☑ **Avoid standing behind a podium**—use effective body language by standing erect and tall and keeping arm gestures between your waist and shoulder.

☑ **Use simple language.** Words with two or more syllables are more difficult to understand.

"Speaking and communicating is a big part of a career these days," Charney says. "Nothing will enhance your career more than showing your expertise through a speech."

———◆———

Love the Speech, Hate the Tie

You've practiced your presentation until even the family dog heads for cover when he hears your opening line. You've researched your data, your handouts are ready, the slides have been double-checked and now the big moment is near.

Time to give your big presentation that will hopefully rank right up there with The Gettysburg Address and catapult you into the career stratosphere. But wait a minute. You're not going to wear that tie, are you? And your hair—are you sure?

Unfortunately, it is a fact of life that while you're giving your presentation, many people will be mentally checking out your clothes, your hair, the spinach stuck in your teeth. And if they find anything about your appearance distracting, you can kiss your presentation's success good-bye.

Because, as communications expert Karen Kalish will tell you, "no matter what you say, your clothes say more."

Kalish, a former network reporter and communications expert, has some tips on how to dress for your presentation and speech so that your message gets through:[6]

☑ **Dress like your audience or one step above.** That means if everyone is in black tie, then you should be, too. If it's a more casual setting, then wear more relaxed clothing, perhaps with a jacket. If you're unsure, think about who your audience is going to be. If it's a bunch of bankers and lawyers, then a conservative suit is a good bet. More creative folks like artists or advertisers would be okay with something a little jazzier, but just make sure it doesn't go overboard. Remember you don't want to distract anyone with your clothing.

☑ **Even minor details are important.** Find a mirror before you confront your audience and comb your hair, freshen your makeup, straighten your tie. If you've got on dangling earrings, a wild tie, a flashy scarf or a rumpled suit, your audience will be distracted. Take off a nametag and tuck it in a pocket until the presentation is over.

☑ **For men, a charcoal gray or blue suit or sport coat is best— no black.** Wear a long-sleeve white shirt, unless television cameras are present. Then select light gray or light blue, which will help prevent you from looking washed out. If you button your coat, make sure that the lapels lie flat. If they don't, then leave the coat undone, and avoid vests. (They add pounds.)

Find a conservative, even boring, tie. Striped red or maroon is good. And if you're going to be seated at any time, find socks that reach high enough that no one has to see a slice of hairy leg. Black or brown shined shoes are a good idea, and make sure there are no holes in your soles.

If you wear jewelry, only use a watch and a ring. No tie pins, lapel pins, earrings or necklaces.

☑ **For women, avoid pastel or pale-colored suits or dresses since bolder colors will make you look strong and confident.** (A pastel blouse with a strong suit is okay, and best if there are television cameras. White blouses should be used otherwise.) If you are going to be sitting where others can see your legs before or after the presentation, keep your skirt length at knee- to mid-calf length. Shoes should have moderate heels with closed toes. Carry an extra pair of hose for emergencies.

Keep your jewelry simple and conservative. Pearls or gold look fine, but avoid diamonds and large, chunky or dangling necklaces, bracelets or earrings. Avoid low necklines, heavy makeup and black clothing—Kalish says it adds 10 years to your age.

You Didn't Wear *That,* Did You?

Forget the shaky worldwide markets, the CEOs that make zillions while employees face the constant threat of layoffs, and the pressures to juggle personal and professional demands. Those things don't really add up to a hill of beans when you get people talking about what really bugs them in the workplace today: the way we dress.

Bosses complain that workers have overstepped the bounds of "casual dress" and show up in clothing better suited to mowing the lawn or hitting the bars on Friday night. Employees complain that they dress fine, but co-workers have absolutely no fashion sense and it hurts just to look at them. Customers say they can't enjoy a meal when being served by someone with a pierced tongue.

The key to this uproar, says a career strategist, is for everyone to simply "dress appropriately."

"If it's going to offend even a small part of any group—co-workers or customers—then it's not appropriate," says Marilyn Moats Kennedy, a business newsletter publisher.

Agrees Nadine Grant, a communications consultant: "We've accepted more casual dress in the workplace, but now people are breaking those rules as well. If clothing—or the lack of it—is distracting, then that's not good business sense."

Kennedy says the key to your dress habits should be your customers. "You are supposed to make your customers think of you as a professional. If it makes anyone uncomfortable—including co-workers—then you shouldn't wear it."

And while many employers may not care what you wear if you do not meet with anyone during the day and "as long as all the relevant body parts are covered," Kennedy says, there are some guidelines you can use when dressing casually and seeing others throughout the day. Among them:

☑ **No "revealing" clothes.** That means no muscle shirts, no shorts, no low-cut blouses or sun dresses for women. And, for those who seem to need a reminder, appropriate undergarments are required. And in this category, (unless you are a cast member of "Ally McBeal"), too tight and too short are also no-nos.

☑ **Be clean.** No, you cannot wear those pants for the fifth day in a row after they've been thrown on the floor each night. Make sure your clothes are clean, and are not so wrinkled it looks like you slept in them.

☑ **Watch the denim.** Some workplaces may say denim is okay, but the problem is too many people take advantage and show up in jeans they last wore to plow the north 40. Denim does not look professional on anyone, so it's better to stick with khaki pants.

☑ **Decent shoes.** Sandals are okay if you've given yourself a pedicure. ("I don't want to look at your dirty, unkempt toes, and neither does anyone else," Kennedy says.) Leave the grubby tennis shoes at home.

☑ **Keep piercing at a minimum.** Kennedy tells the story of how she was in a restaurant and it literally made her feel sick when she looked at the server who had a pierced tongue. Thinking it was only offensive to someone her age, Kennedy was quickly assured by her daughter (age 17), that "it almost made her sick too."

Pierced ears are okay for work—but leave other pierced body parts undecorated until after work.

And, if you still don't believe your dress should influence your career, keep in mind that Americans may understand your need to wear your tie-dyed T-shirt five days a week, but other people may not.

"In some cultures, Americans are perceived as being disrespectful because of the way we dress to do business. We're always judged by how we look—and whether that's right or wrong—it's the truth," Grant says.

Got That Report Here Somewhere

Quick: Grab a pen, a clean notepad of paper, the report you worked on over the weekend and a calendar.

How long did it take you to do that? A minute? An hour? Still looking?

Barbara Hemphill, a professional organizer for nearly two decades, has seen it all—paper piles of gargantuan proportions and filing systems that scream for mercy. And she has calmly imparted her wisdom and organizational wizardry to those who truly want to see the tops of their desks again.

"There's an old adage about a place for everything and everything in its place," Hemphill says. "Well, that's only half true. Because I know very few people who have the discipline to work with only one thing on their desk at a time."

Hemphill says that stress about a messy existence comes not from the clutter itself, but from the fear of filing something away and then not being able to find it when needed. She counsels the faint-hearted to practice the "art of wastebasketry," which means deciding what really is needed, and what can be dumped in the nearest trash can or recycling bin.

And she shows little mercy for that pile of paper balancing precariously against another pile on your desk. Those piles, she says, represent nothing more than your inability to make decisions. And—brace yourself—she says that 40 percent of the contents of an "in basket" can be thrown away. Only 20 percent, she says, demands immediate attention, while the remaining 40 percent can be filed.

"Ask yourself what's the worst possible thing that can happen if you throw that piece of paper away," she says. "In some cases, it might be the exact thing you'll need, so you'll file it. But if not, throw it away."

Why does there seem to be so much paper and clutter in our lives these days? Believe it or not, the computer is to blame.

"Computers come with printers," Hemphill says. "And now people print out all on-line stuff and e-mail. We have fax machines that generate paper that we have to sort through. Now, in addition to everything else, we have to organize the technology."

Further, Hemphill says today's filing systems are a disgrace, because there is so much duplication. She advocates making a list of file names, then consulting that list before creating new files. As for computer clutter, she advises that one-time documents be zapped into never-never land rather than kept on file in a computer's system.

So, if you're tired of your office being declared a fire hazard (or health hazard, depending on the depth of your messiness), then here are a few tips from Hemphill:[7]

☑ **If it is difficult to "let go" of clutter, think of somewhere it might be happier.** For example, books can be donated to a local library or school.

☑ **Today's mail is tomorrow's pile.** Forget the backlog until you get today's mail under control.

☑ **Use one calendar as a reference for important appointments and meetings.**

☑ **Track what materials pile up most frequently and seek ways to eliminate the constant problem.**

☑ **Use desktops for items that are used daily or weekly.**

☑ **Try to create enough room on your desk so that you may comfortably spread out your arms.**

☑ **If you can't face the mess yourself, contact the National Association of Professional Organizers** in Austin, Texas (512-206-0151), which can give you a member's name in your area to help you.

———●———

You're Going to Have to Check That Bag, Ma'am

Remember what your briefcase looked like the first time you saw it? It was shiny, sleek, reeking of professionalism and smelling of new leather.

Now, take a good hard look at it. Bulging, battered, shapeless, crammed with papers and a cell phone and the lunch you forgot to eat yesterday. And—are those tire tracks on its side?

Now, try and find anything in it quickly without dumping the entire contents on the floor.

Briefcases have become the "mini-offices" in our lives, often a condition made much worse if we're on the road. After traveling to five cities in three nights, we've shoved business cards and brochures and meeting schedules in our satchels to the point that skeptical airline agents claim it will never fit under the seat, let alone an overhead bin.

So this once-proud briefcase now becomes the symbol of all that is wrong with business travel these days—disorganization away from the office that now leads to even more disorganization once we return.

Because if you're like most people, when you return to the office you're going to be faced with a desk piled high with work, phone messages marked "urgent" and a personal life demanding whatever energy you have left. And the reality is that your conference material will get shoved into a corner, your contact names will be dumped in a desk drawer and you will end up paying for part of your trip out of your own pocket because you can't remember how much you tipped the bellhop or find the receipt from lunch.

There are ways, however, to stay in control of your road travels by using some simple strategies that mirror good organizational techniques in an office.

Barbara Hemphill, an organizational guru, says the biggest mistake business travelers make is not creating the proper systems that deal with on-the-road needs.

"For example, turn your briefcase into a mini-desk," she says. "In your briefcase, have a file that is marked 'to file.' Carry a copy of your file index from the office with you so you can check the list and know just how to label everything you want to keep. Jot in the right-hand corner of each piece of paper what action you want to take."

Hemphill stresses that the key to controlling on-the-road clutter is to make decisions as you go. To cut down on the amount of paper collected, carry pre-addressed envelopes that can be filled with information you want to keep, then mailed back to your office. Ideally, someone at the office can then file these according to your notations. If not, at least you've already sorted through the paper and it only has to be filed when you return.

Here are some other tips from Hemphill:[8]

☑ **Make your briefcase user friendly.** "I always want my briefcase to open from the top so that I don't have to put it down in order to open it," she says. "I always have an outside zipper pocket for my keys and airline tickets." Further, she uses a large envelope with the flap tucked in as a sort of "pocket" inside the briefcase so she can easily pop in receipts and other vital scraps of paper.

☑ **Keep up with expense reports.** It's really a good idea to fill them out daily—while waiting for your plane, sitting in traffic or over breakfast at your hotel. That way, it's less likely you'll forget what you tipped the cab driver or that it cost you $2 for a lemon wedge at a swank restaurant.

☑ **Organize your business cards.** Use one pocket for your own business cards, another for those you collect. When making a contact, write the date and place on the business card, and don't hesitate to pitch those you know you'll never need. If you're not going to take action on the contact, enter the card into a file or computer program by using a key retrieval word—something that comes to mind when thinking of the person.

☑ **Write thank-you notes as you go**. A hurried note is better than none at all. Keep a list so you won't duplicate your efforts or forget one.

☑ **Remember being organized on the road doesn't happen without being organized at home.**

Better Mind Your Own Beeswax

The report was just sitting there, almost under your nose. Okay, so it was on the boss's desk and you were sitting a few feet away, but you have really good eyesight—and the ability to read upside down—so it wasn't really your fault you read a co-worker's recent performance evaluation, was it? Just like it didn't really mean anything when you and another co-worker gossiped over lunch about the trouble brewing in accounting?

This all may seem harmless—you're just keeping up on what's going on after all—but it points out that the American workplace needs some confidentiality guidelines. How would you like it if someone were trying to get a glimpse at your last performance evaluation, or was dishing the latest dirt about your spat with a manager?

Chances are it would make you uncomfortable, and probably a little angry. While we may like to see every detail of a person's life exposed on daily talk shows, it's another matter when it's our lives being discussed. And that's exactly what is landing many employers in court these days. Workers who are upset that their rights have been violated by their personal lives being exposed on the job are suing companies in record numbers—and winning.

But where exactly should we draw the line between confidences and just friendly chit-chat? The answer to that may depend on what position you hold in a company, and what information you are discussing, and with whom.

Donald Weiss, a management consultant who often lectures and writes on the law and personnel matters, admits that there is a "fine line" between private information and "just getting to know one another."

Some cases seem pretty clear cut. For example, Weiss says there was a woman who told her boss she was HIV-positive and would need some time off for treatments. She asked her supervisor to keep that information confidential, but he told human resources—and that landed the manager in legal hot water.

"You must always look at who has the privilege—the right or the need to know certain types of information," Weiss says. "That right is usually qualified or conditional, limited to the immediate and legitimate concerns or interests of the parties involved. Not everyone has a right or need to know everything about everyone."

Weiss cautions that while it is often managers who are dragged through the legal system, employees should also be aware of sticky issues, and carefully read their company handbooks to find out what they may or may not discuss. For some employers, it is taboo to talk about salaries with other workers, while some companies now consider all e-mail to be company property. That means workers are not allowed to send personal e-mail messages.

And while that may lead us to be a bit paranoid about behaving openly in the workplace, Weiss says it's no reason to go overboard. He says that workers are more productive and satisfied if they get to know other employees better, and employers usually share that view. He advises that each person should simply keep in mind that everyone deserves dignity and privacy—and that should temper our actions.

With that in mind, here are some ways to improve confidentiality in the workplace:

1. **During conference calls, make sure each person is identified before beginning a conversation.** Ask that if anyone joins in later they be immediately identified.

2. **Only send e-mails after double-checking the address.** Send messages with the thought that they could be read by several other employees. Are you comfortable with what you have written?

3. **Do not discuss your salary or anyone else's** unless it's part of your collective bargaining agreement.

4. **When making a phone call, clearly identify who is on the other end before speaking,** and always identify yourself, even if you are calling a familiar number.

5. **Do not attempt to get the boss's spouse alone at the next office party and gain information.** In fact, don't talk company business with a spouse or significant other of any employee or manager.

6. **If you're discussing company business, always be aware of who is around you and who could overhear.** Don't let anyone sneak up behind you—you might even go so far as to never sit with your back to the door when in conference or a private conversation.

7. **Lock your desk and your files during lunch or at the end of the day,** or when you're going to be away for a certain amount of time, such as in a meeting. Take precautions to protect your computer information by keeping your password in your head—not written down somewhere.

8. **Use a paper shredder,** and avoid putting confidential information into the recycling bin if it has not been shredded first.

9. **When receiving internal mail, always make sure your name is on the front before opening,** even if it was hand-delivered to you.

10. **Unless you receive a supervisor's permission, do not allow anyone to have access to information that you consider confidential.**

11. **Resist discussing a co-worker's troubles** (personal or professional) with another employee, even if you do it out of "concern."

Keep the Mayo Cold, and the Thong Bikini in the Closet

Business entertaining can be one of the most nerve-wracking experiences in a professional life. Deciding who to invite, what to serve, what to wear and what to talk about can cause many sleepless nights, since one social gaffe can stick in the minds of business associates for years.

And if you decide to do that entertaining at your home, then you need to worry about a few more things, such as keeping your St. Bernard from slobbering on your boss, or making sure the potato salad hasn't gone bad, causing co-workers to throw up in the azaleas.

"A mistake in business entertainment is something that no one forgets, no matter how small it is," says Suzanne Williamson, who gives seminars on business entertaining. "You've got to plan your function well and be organized."

Williamson says that if you decide to entertain at home, then one of the first things you must consider is the seating arrangements—letting guests sit "randomly" is a no-no.

"You've got to get it absolutely right. Figure out why each person is there, and then sit them next to people who make sense, such as putting a new client next to the person wanting their business," Williamson says. "Also, don't sit two competitors next to each other, and remember to always seat guests according to rank whenever possible."[9]

Other ideas:

☑ **Be clear on your invitations about what dress is required.** Saying "casual" doesn't cut it, since that can mean anything from shorts to a silk pantsuit. Williamson says if you're a guest, it's always better to overdress, or carry a swimsuit in a small bag until you make sure that everyone else is going into the pool. "And let me emphasize this: Don't wear revealing clothing, ever. You want to be remembered for your intelligence and good ideas, not your cleavage," she says.

☑ **Get moral support.** If you're hosting a business dinner at your home, also consider inviting some good friends, who can be trusted to keep the conversation moving, and provide a fun and enjoyable atmosphere. Williamson says most business associates enjoy meeting new people, and look forward to a social gathering that is relaxing and not focused solely on the bottom line.

"Most people don't want to spend their time away from the office talking only about business. So find out about each of your guests—their hobbies, their family, what they enjoy doing. Then you can ask them questions. Remember, the best thing is to be a good listener and let your guests do all the talking," Williamson says.

☑ **Let guests see you in your natural habitat.** Williamson says it's okay to let your children participate in business entertaining, especially if they're old enough to help with clearing a table, or can be depended on to provide interesting and polite conversation during dinner. If, however, your children are young, it might be a good idea to let them stay a short while and then have a baby-sitter take them elsewhere for the rest of the time.

The same cannot be said of pets, however. Many people dislike having anything shed, slobber or sit on them, so it's best to have the dog or cat comfortably settled out of the way, she says.

☑ **Don't sweat the setting.** "When you entertain at home, don't worry so much about what your house looks like, unless it's a disgusting mess and then you need to decide if you can clean it up enough to have people over," Williamson says. "But really, for business entertainment, most people like sitting at the kitchen table eating simple, good, food. Don't fuss with a bunch of fancy dishes, because your job is to concentrate on your guests."

☑ **Ask for reinforcements.** Williamson says that if you can afford it, a caterer can be a big help as long as food is still kept simple, and a bartender can be told when to cut off the bar so that guests are sober when it comes time to drive home. "You should serve only quality liquor or wine at your home, but also have lots of water and juice available so that people don't overdo it," she says. "Still, don't hesitate to call a cab or drive someone home if you believe they've had too much to drink."

Finally, Williamson advises that if you do make a mistake, no matter how small, try to handle it with humor. Then, apologize again by sending a note or flowers to your guests so that their final memory of entertainment in your home is one of style, grace and fun.

Is It Time For a Life Yet?

There are different responses from people when asking what is lacking in life these days. Some may say money, others may note they don't have a job they enjoy or complain they don't have a meaningful personal relationship.

Still, if you ask people if they are always short on time, you probably will receive a resounding and unanimous "yes!"

Experts say that we feel the time crunch so severely we're even giving up sleep in a desperate bid to find more time to get everything done. But even that doesn't seem to catch us up, so now we're still not getting it all done, and we're exhausted to boot.

And yet time management experts argue that there really is enough time to get done everything we would like, and get a good night's rest. The key: taking a hard look at your life, and determining what you really want to do.

Then—and this may be the toughest part—letting the other stuff go. That may sound simplistic, but Shirley Long says that by taking this attitude, we truly can find a way to get our work done and still have lives with family and friends.

Long has worked closely with time management guru Alec Mackenzie on books and videotapes, and says there are many time-wasters in our lives at work, from ringing telephones to drop-in visitors to an inability to say no. And it seems that every day more are added to the list, including time hassles for the self-employed (reams of paperwork for the government) and additional headaches caused by technology (think of the useless e-mails you've received in the last week.)

"We are in a time trap zoo these days," Long says. "We are in an age of unlimited possibility, and we want to do everything. But what kind of life is that? You run around like a chicken with its head cut off."

To avoid such problems, Long says there are a number of steps you can take to tackle your time-wasters.[10] Among them:

- ☑ **Make clear choices.** Take a hard look at what you want to accomplish, then write it down. Post that note where you can see it every day, and use it to guide you in your decisions. If someone approaches you with an idea, you can quickly consult your list and see if it fits. If not, politely and cheerfully tell the person "no." Be honest, be matter of fact—but be firm.

- ☑ **Stop interruptions.** One of the biggest time-wasters starts with "Hi. Got a minute?" No, you really don't. So when someone drops in on you at work, and the visit cannot be handled quickly (immediately ask what the visit is about), set up another time to talk, refer the visitor to someone else, or simply be honest and tell the visitor—or friend—that you're in the middle of something. You can chat with friends over lunch, and colleagues will understand when you're on a deadline or in the middle of an important project.

- ☑ **Learn to say "no."** Are you one of those people who says "yes" when someone makes a request, then you mentally kick yourself in the behind? Next time, when a request catches you off guard, don't say anything until you count to 10. By listening carefully, you can understand what is being asked of you, and then give a firm "no." If it's appropriate, you can give the reasons for your negative answer, but don't offer any reasons if they are just wishy-washy excuses. You can always show your good faith by offering alternatives.

Saying "no" becomes a bit trickier when the request is made by your boss. In that case, review whether the request falls under your agreed-upon priorities. If the boss insists, then go ahead, but state what you fear will not get done because of it.

☑ **Start delegating.** First, get your ego out of the way; it is usually heavily involved when you can't let other people help you out. If they don't do the job to your satisfaction, they'll learn. If they do it better than you, the entire organization wins. Mistakes can and will be made, but that's part of business, and part of learning. If someone else can do the task, make the best match you can (it may not be perfect), give delegates clear instructions, allow them the authority to accomplish tasks and be there to support and coach as needed.

☑ **Handle change.** When we consider using technology, we must decide how knowledgeable we need to become, and how much mastery of the subject we can delegate to others. We also need to look at how much we can master to find solutions quickly on our own, or whether it would be better to track what is needed through other sources.

At the same time, consider what works best on paper, what needs to be done electronically and where you need to interact personally.

☑ **Get organized.** So much time is wasted each day looking for things that have been lost. At the end of the day, take time to organize, evaluate and plan for the next day.

"If you don't make time management decisions, other people will decide, the environment will decide, or accidents will decide," Long says. "Time management is critical. If you don't get it under control, you will drown.

No human being can achieve an infinite number of goals, so make your choices and live with them."

—•—

Stick 'Em Up: What's Your Personal Mission Statement?

Say you're at a business cocktail party, mingling with other professionals while juggling a cheesepuff and a glass of white wine in one hand while shaking hands with the other.

You find yourself in a group where the talk turns to spiritual issues. Do you pretend to choke on the cheesepuff and make quick getaway, or do you join in the discussion?

Experts say that the smart response would be to stick around and listen. Because even if it makes you uncomfortable, spirituality is taking hold in the workplace.

Why? There are many opinions on the matter, but some contend that workers who feel less confident about their future and often combat anger, depression and frustration are looking for something to help them feel that what they are doing in life is worthwhile. Workplace chaplains are becoming more commonplace, and some employers actually encourage employees to form spiritual groups at work.

And even those who do not practice a specific religion find that spiritual teachings can help them find a clearer career path. That doesn't surprise Laurie Beth Jones, an author and speaker on workplace spirituality.

"If you're in harmony with your divine source," Jones says, "your life will be much more fulfilled and fulfilling."

Jones often cites the teachings of spiritual leaders such as Jesus Christ, but contends that each person is spiritual in an individual way, and must use that spirituality to find purpose in and out of the workplace.

"Spirituality is here. It is an innate part of people," she says. "And in the workplace, there is a need to have our gifts used and acknowledged."

Jones stresses that as part of this movement, people should have a personal mission statement—much like Jesus Christ who "constantly and publicly proclaimed his mission and then stuck to it—the key to his success."

She says that an individual's personal mission statement should:[11]

☑ **Be no more than a single sentence.**

☑ **Be easily understood by a 12-year-old.**

☑ **Be easy to recite by memory at gunpoint.**

Sound tough to do? Not really. Think of other mission statements through the generations. "Abraham Lincoln's mission was the preserve the Union…Nelson Mandela's mission was to end apartheid," Jones says. "Joan of Arc's mission was to save France."

Once you have a mission statement, then you must work to make it successful. First, thoroughly research the facts behind your mission statement. Investigate, ask questions and then continually update your information before taking action.

Next:

☑ **Boil your mission down to the single most important task or goal.** Write it down and communicate it to others so that they can repeat it word for word.

☑ **Look at the resources at hand and use them wisely.** Educate others about your mission and let them know what's in it for them.

☑ **Use contacts from the past to help you** and consider what dreams or talents you once had that can be "reawakened."

☑ **Stop marching in place.** Be bold—break ranks.

☑ **Begin and end all missions with prayer.**

"Knowing your personal mission statement is the best career insurance you could ever have," Jones says. "Once you know what you were put here to do, then a job is only a means toward your mission, not an end in itself."

Aunt Bea, We Need You

Do you consider yourself to be an honest person? Are you truthful, honorable and stick to the high road? Even at work?

According to those who have seen what the business world has to offer, the nicest folks are not populating the corporate hallways. In fact, we have become a nation of what business consultant Rob Lebow calls "competitive liars."

"Our world is rudderless because we're constantly seduced by the size of our business and the money involved," he says. "Every now and then we have values—then we somehow always get derailed. It's not loud and obvious when it happens, like a train wreck. It's more like some quiet, insidious change."

Lebow contends there are eight basic people values needed in the workplace today:[12]

1. **Treating others with uncompromising truth.** Always discuss the truth with a person within 24 hours, and begin with, "Is this a good time to talk?" And, because no one ever said telling the truth was easy, ask the other person's permission to tell the truth before beginning. Don't apologize for the truth and be nonthreatening.

2. **Lavishing trust on your associates.** Make it clear from the beginning what you expect, agree when the job should be done, be completely supportive and trust the other person to complete the task, despite the challenges you see them face. If you want to gain trust in return, agree to the task, put the request in your own words and ask for help if you need it.

3. **Mentoring unselfishly.** Before beginning, get the other person's permission, then share knowledge, skills and experience in a friendly way. Make sure you put the other person's interest before your own. If you want to be mentored, give your permission, be open to new ideas and show a willingness to be mentored by everyone in the organization.

4. **Being receptive to new ideas.** Listen with an open mind, be nonjudgemental, ask questions and provide a follow-up.

5. **Taking personal risks for the good of the organization.** Be willing to share ideas, even if they're unpopular. Speak up even if there's a chance you might be wrong. And if you're right? Forge ahead. At the same time, you must support others when they step forward with their ideas and don't forget to use your common sense so your actions are appropriate to the situation.

6. **Giving credit.** Be honest and straightforward with praise and make sure it's given while the job is happening. Cut the criticism and instead use positive statements about what you want. Make sure feedback is timely and appropriate when actions aren't up to individual or group standards.

7. **Being honest in all dealings.** Lebow likes to tell the story (later to become a Harvard University case study on ethics) of how when he worked at Microsoft Corporation he was trying to choose a new ad agency while preparing to launch a new product that was a direct challenge to a Lotus Corporation flagship product. It seems one agency thought to woo Microsoft business by telling Lebow trade secrets about Lotus. Lebow's reaction was immediate: he reported the unethical conduct to company lawyers who then forwarded it to Lotus.

8. **Putting the interests of others before your own.** Root for others' success, even if there's nothing in it for you. Finally, support others and yourself by acting upon the organization's values every day.

"I don't think it's the churches or schools that are going to make the biggest change in our world today," Lebow says. "The playing field is the office. Even if you work at home, the biggest issue is still work. If we follow these values, it's the door through which you want to go, it's the room in which you want to stay."

NOTES

[1] M.W. Mercer, *How Winners Do It* (Wellington Publishers, 1988)

[2] Norbert Aubuchon, *The Anatomy of Persuasion* (Amacom, 1997)

[3] Stephanie G. Sherman with V. Clayton Sherman, *Make Yourself Memorable* (Amacom)

[4] Tony Alessandra, *Charisma* (Warner, 1998)

[5] Cy Charney, *The Manager's Tool Kit* (Amacom, 1995)

[6] Karen Kalish, *How to Give a Terrific Presentation* (Amacom, 1997)

[7] Barbara Hemphill, *Taming the Office Tiger* (Kiplinger, 1996)

[8] Barbara Hemphill, *Taming the Office Tiger* (Kiplinger, 1996)

[9] Suzanne Williamson, *Entertaining for Dummies* (IDG Books, 1997)

[10] Alex Mackenzie, *Time Trap* (Amacom, 1997, 1990)

[11] Laurie Beth Jones, *The Path* (Hyperion, 1996)

[12] Rob Lebow and William L. Simon, *Lasting Change* (Van Nostrand Reinhold, 1997)

2

WORK ENVIRONMENT

I grew up in a small town in Oklahoma that had two movie theaters. One was known for its rodent population, and the other played Grease for an entire summer. There wasn't always a lot going on to entertain teenagers (the lament of young people everywhere), so it was interesting that this small town boasted a zoo.

From what I can remember, it wasn't a big zoo. It had a big monkey "pit" in the middle, where playful animals scampered about, and there was the prairie dog display that consisted of some dirt and some prairie dogs. Then, of course, there was the buffalo.

I'm not sure if this buffalo was native. Since thousands once roamed the great plains of the state at one time, I assume that if he wasn't from the exact area, he at least had to be kin of some who were.

Anyway, I doubt most people have actually smelled a buffalo, but they stink pretty bad. I'm not sure if stink even begins to describe it. Old sneakers stink. This fellow made your eyes water if you got within 50 feet of his pen.

And, he also was pretty surly. I'm not sure buffalo are supposed to have congenial personalities, but this one sure didn't. I believe much of that was due to the fact he was penned up at the edge of a zoo, instead of running free as his ancestors once did.

41

So it was that when you approached his pen, or even cast your eyes in his direction, he would become agitated and start stirring up the dirt in his pen. And, being Oklahoma where the wind never stops blowing, the smell of an irate buffalo would begin to drift throughout a nearby park—where they annually held a ceremony for high school seniors.

It's amazing how one unhappy buffalo can ruin the whole day.

Eventually the town got rid of the zoo. I've always wondered what happened to that buffalo. I hope he's stomping the great prairie in the sky, but all I know is that park is a much nicer place to be now that he's gone.

Now, you may wonder about the point of this story, but I believe that we could learn a thing or two from that old buffalo.

Think about it: at work, if there is just one unhappy person, they pretty much stink up the whole joint, don't they? If the boss is a grouch, that ruins everyone's job, doesn't it? Or if people simply cannot work together creatively and enthusiastically, it can make going to work kind of like smelling a bad bison all day.

That's why it's critical—for productivity, efficiency and bottom-line success—that the work environment be as pleasant as possible. Mostly, this means people have to get along by relying on the strengths each person brings to the table, and by not condemning people because they don't fit the mold we believe they should.

It also means that we have to accept issues like generational or cultural differences. Generation X—those born between 1963 and 1977—have much to offer. They're innovative, creative and technologically savvy, but have been called "slackers" by older workers. That stinks. Just like it stinks when we believe workers 50 and older should be nudged out the door, or that we have nothing to learn from the corporate-savvy Baby Boomers.

Unlike the buffalo, we have a choice. We don't have to be trapped in a pen, but can make work a place we'd like to be, make some decisions that will not only make going to work good for us, but nice for others also.

Fire Up the Barbeque, Boss

The phones are ringing off the hook, just like they have been all day. You've dealt with irate customers, soothed suppliers half a world away and have taken only one break all day, and that was because you drank half a pot of coffee, and well, you just had to take care of "business" before moving to the next stressful situation.

Then, suddenly the phones stop ringing. You see the guy next to you pull out a golf club. The woman across the room strolls by with some golf balls. Pretty soon everyone else heads for the hallway. You follow.

And there, in front of the boss and everybody, a putting contest is hotly under way. Your co-workers are laughing, placing bets on who has the best chance of winning. Some balls are hit too hard and shoot past the cup that is really an old coffee mug. There's more laughter and pretty soon the winner is rewarded by being allowed to buy everyone a cold soda.

The whole thing has lasted 20 minutes, and you figure you'll wake up from this dream pretty soon.

But then the phones start ringing again, and you realize you feel better than you have all day. The tension between your shoulders has eased, there's a lingering smile on your lips, and now you're enjoying a cold drink delivered to your desk by a smirking woman holding a gold club!

What is it? What has happened? Well, it's not a dream. It's called, simply, fun.

Experts in fun (yes, there are some), contend that the American workplace is sadly lacking in having a good time. And if you think that is a joke, consider that there are managers at even the most conservative companies who are serving pancakes breakfasts to employees, flipping burgers at a lunch barbecue or washing the windshield of a deserving worker.

People on the job, faced with never-ending stress, are turning off the phones for short breaks, pitching pennies in the hallway, holding a paper airplane contest outside on a nice day—and having putting contests in the hall.

Still, no one ever said work was supposed to be fun, so what gives?

"Things have definitely changed," says Jim Harris, a management consultant. "It's no longer a case of someone applying for a job and trying to get a company excited about hiring them by telling them what they can do for the company. It's a whole new ballgame. Now employees are telling employers that if you want me—but can't always promise me that I'll have this job—then you've got to do something to make me want to work for you."

Harris says that the most successful companies are taking the focus away from making a profit, "because they've become tremendously good at that," and looking at the "profit-makers"—the employees.

Harris has come up with a number of ways employees can have fun on the job,[1] and so have other fun gurus such as Matt Weinstein,[2] including:

☑ **Creating a "stress-free" zone.** Stocked with comfortable furniture (one company used a hammock) and maybe even provide a punching bag in case someone needs to vent a little frustration.

☑ **Romping like children.** Playing marbles, shooting a few hoops outside at a company-provided basketball goal or even tossing a baseball back and forth can last for as few as 15 minutes while voice-mail handles the phones.

☑ **When watching a training film, having popcorn and snacks.** Then rating the film "thumbs up" or "thumbs down."

☑ **Bringing a personal life to work.** With many workers facing eldercare issues, it's a good time to bring aging parents in, serve them tea and cookies and let them see what a good job the kid is doing. Or, pets can be great stress relievers as long as they are well behaved and other workers don't object.

☑ **Taking advantage of nice weather.** Set up some tables outside, serve lunch or hot fudge sundaes, have a watermelon seed spitting contest. Serve strawberry shortcake, or even order pizza. Just make sure it's all served by the boss.

☑ **Paying for someone's parking, or having their car washed.** Try sending them flowers or balloons, or just letting them have the day off.

☑ **Having a ugly shoe or ugly tie contest.** Dressing up for Halloween, or having an "Elvis" party on The King's birthday.

Even Obnoxious Twits Can Be Charmed

You wake up one morning and discover that you'd like to whip up a nice cream pie—maybe three or four. You're not planning on eating them of course. You'd like to just take them to the office, then calmly plant them in the faces of a few co-workers.

The people at work are driving you crazy. Every annoying habit, every word they utter is like scraping fingernails across a blackboard. This, my friend, is a sign that you need a vacation.

But if you can't get away just now, and fear that you may really throw your stapler at the idiot sitting near you, then it's time for an attitude adjustment—yours.

First, remember that we are required to work more closely together at work these days, especially because teams are used for everything from constructing a jet engine to choosing toilet paper. That's why it's important you learn to put your personal frustrations aside and work with people, even if they qualify as obnoxious twits or old grumps in your book.

Cherie Carter-Scott, who has made a career out of addressing negative behavior in the workplace, says that nastiness on the job has increased with downsizings and layoffs over the last decade. Those have caused increased pressures and stress on the people "who fear that if they don't get the work done, then they will get sacked," she says.

Even workers who have held positive views and been pleasant to work with in the past can be sucked into having gloom and doom feelings after they have watched numerous peers get the pink slip.

"A normal person can be shattered by these experiences," Carter-Scott says. "So they're spending time grumbling and complaining instead of working."

But there are ways to redirect negative energies in the workplace, and get on nicer terms with peers. Among them:

- ☑ **Treat your co-worker like a customer.** Say "please" and "thank you" and try to be positive when speaking with them.

- ☑ **Relax together.** If a co-worker rejects going out for some social time after work, then order pizza and ask them to share it with you at lunch. Try to get a group together to go to a restaurant.

☑ **Look for the differences.** Life would be pretty boring if everyone were the same. New ideas and new ways of looking at issues can get creative juices flowing. Learn to appreciate the diversity instead of resenting it.

☑ **Be genuine.** There's nothing more stomach-turning than mumbling a "Hihowyadoing" greeting as you pass someone. Take the time to look a co-worker in the eye, greet them and smile. If you ask a question, wait to hear their response.

☑ **Don't get mad.** When a co-worker is angry, don't respond in kind. Keep your voice level, and say something like, "I can't blame you…I'd feel the same way." Hostile co-workers often lack the ability to trust. By not overreacting, you not only feel more in control and less trapped by that person, but the angry co-worker may learn to reach out in other ways when trouble occurs.

Carter-Scott also suggests that each day you should do something nice for yourself that shows you are worthwhile. It can range from having dinner at a nice restaurant, to watching a sunset, to taking a long walk and stopping to smell the flowers. And, each night before you go to bed, write down all the good news of the day. This might be something as simple as a co-worker who shared a funny joke, to volunteering for a project at you're child's school, to seeing a beautiful butterfly on your lunch break.

The point is, positive energy from you can infect others in the workplace. That means by being good to yourself, you will feel more like being good to others—and that will be returned to you. And then everyone on the job wins.

Snipers and Tanks Roaming Office Hallways

One of the keys to handling workplace conflicts may be your ability to recognize a tank. You know about the military kind, rolling over any obstruction in its path. There's also the human kind—rolling over any obstruction in its path.

A "tank" is a pushy or aggressive person, someone who should put you on full alert to guard your emotions and reactions. A "sniper" on the other hand, attempts to get his or her own way by embarrassing or humiliating you, while a "know-it-all" dominates conversations with lengthy, imperious arguments and likes to discredit others by pointing out flaws and weaknesses.

Sound familiar? Like a few people you work with every day?

It's these personality types—and a few choice others—that make work environments so stressful, says Dr. Rick Kirshner, who often writes and lectures about these conflicts with fellow naturopathic physician Dr. Rick Brinkman.

"Stress brings with it the 'fight or flight' response," Kirshner says. "What you have to learn is how to understand those responses."[3]

For example, Kirshner says that when dealing with the "tank" you can't simply defend or justify your position, or shut down, because it probably won't work. Instead, you must stand your ground, and interrupt by calmly saying the person's name several times. Then, quickly backtrack the main point by showing you heard and understood the accusations, then move on to the bottom line. Outline how you think the outcome can be achieved.

He also recommends:

☑ **Being aggressive** and direct with a "sniper" who needs to be brought out of hiding. If you get a snide comment, address the sniper's jibe. Keep your tone neutral and have an innocent look on your face. Try asking, "When you say that, what are you really trying to say?"

☑ **Being flexible** with the "know-it-all" and maintain your patience. Be clever about how you present your ideas. Respectfully and sincerely let the person see that you understand the "brilliance" behind his or her opinion. You also can become less of a threat by regarding this person as a mentor, or by beginning your sentences with "maybe" or "perhaps."

☑ **Listening to the "whiner"** no matter how agonizing. These are the folks who complain that nothing is right and there are no solutions. So you must write down the complaints, and interrupt (tactfully) and get specific. Ask for the whiner's help. Then shift the focus to solutions and ask them what they want.

☑ **Dealing positively with the "just say no" person.** It can build character. This is the person who figures nothing can ever go right and who pulls others into the pit of despair. These people often have personal trials that have sunk them to these depths, but what's important is that you not get sucked in with them. Tell yourself that dealing positively with this person builds character. Get a little thrill by throwing them off and saying, "You're doing a wonderful job." Or, use them as an early warning system—let them dissect and destroy every idea to look for flaws.

☑ **Be willing to take more time with the "nothing" person.** This is the person who does exactly... nothing. They do and say nothing when events fail to measure up and completely withdraw in frustration. Ask open-ended questions in an expectant way, requiring more from them. Use humor to break down the silent wall erected by the personality type, or try guessing what the problem is to get a response. Show this person the future by telling them what can happen if they continue to be unresponsive. When they start talking listen carefully but don't interrupt.

Which is On First, Who is On Second

It's no secret that many of us are doing twice—if not three or four times—the amount of work we were doing a few years ago. Downsizings and layoffs and the reliance on "teams" have caused organizations to ask each individual to perform a multitude of tasks, many of them simultaneously.

And, of course, with all that work comes a lot of stress. Trying to find enough hours in the day to complete demanding projects while trying to please bosses and customers is a daunting task.

But Pat Nickerson, a corporate trainer and management expert, says there are ways we can do the work that needs to be done, while maintaining our sanity and pleasing the top brass.

The key, she says, is being able to negotiate and debate with others so that it is clear to everyone what the priorities must be "and what you have going on." Also, she says it is critical that you become an entrepreneur—that you "own" your job and determine what work yields the most value.

Specifically, Nickerson says that each worker should use a calendar or planner to list the top three tasks for a day with the highest risks and pay-offs, weighed against your goals. These tasks, she says, should be scheduled during your best times of the day (some people just don't do mornings well), or when you know you can get the privacy or the technical access you need.

Do not, she warns, schedule anything else until these top three priorities have been allotted time.[4]

Then, try to leave the rest of your schedule loose enough to handle unexpected jobs or other tasks that need attention. Remember not to let any unimportant tasks come between you and the top three achievements.

Nickerson adds that you may be forced to "bump" one of your top tasks, especially if you have more than one job. "Each boss has an intense passion for what he or she does, so you can get a real overload," she says.

If a "bump" occurs, then mark it down. Several bumpy weeks may convince you that your job has changed, to the point that you may see that you need help, or realize that it's only a temporary crisis. And there's always the chance you'll discover things aren't going to change—and you want to get a new career.

Perhaps the best way to gain control over multiple tasks and multiple bosses is Nickerson's suggestion to post a board that everyone can see—either near your worksite or on-line—that shows "requested" jobs on the left side of the board, and "committed" jobs on the right side. By keeping a clear picture, you can see what deadlines need to be negotiated, and what tasks need to be delegated.

"Everyone can see this list and what you have to do," she says. "Your boss has the power to be flexible. You can then clearly lay out what task is committed to be done, and how many hours it is going to take. A senior executive's sole job is to direct people and make decisions. So by showing the board, you look at the list of projects and let them make the decisions about what you can back off from."

And the board serves a couple of other purposes, as well.

"It gives you something to look at when the boss is looking angrily at your face," she says, laughing. "And, other people can look at your workload and not even bother you if they see you don't have any free time."

Nickerson says a worker's hesitancy to negotiate the workload "is what enslaves you."

"What gets mercy is a clear, cogent picture of what you have going on," she says. "If you're too afraid to debate, you default."

———•———

Generation X Making Up New Road Rules

Generation X is an independent breed, which sometimes grates on the nerves of Baby Boomers. This generation, born between 1963 and 1977, has new ideas about what they want from work, and it doesn't include schmoozing the boss in order to get ahead and spending lots of overtime at work—tactics Baby Boomers have used for decades to climb the corporate ladder.

And even though younger workers know what they *don't* want, they are a bit unsure about how to get what they *do* want.

Bruce Tulgan, a Generation X expert, has interviewed hundreds of young people about the way they work today.[5]

"Young people guard their private time, and they make a very clear distinction of who their friends are," Tulgan says. "They are making a new career path for themselves, and it's not about hitching their wagon to a star. It's about thinking of themselves as sole proprietors, seeing themselves as free agents."

Still it's not always easy. It can be lonely, and other generations of workers can be critical, Tulgan says, because they don't understand the new way of thinking.

"Generation X has a tremendous amount of loyalty to individuals, not institutions," Tulgan says. "It's a new terrain of loyalty. They don't want the same old job, paying their dues. There are a lot of young people reinventing success and making it up as they go along."

Tulgan explains that the old idea of "networking" is often a waste of time, since relationships only are beneficial if they offer something to the people involved. He says he understands the confusion of Generation X, but says there are ways to make relationships better in the workplace.

"Young people need to look at relationships as transactional and mutual. They need to think through why they're making a contact," he says.

Tulgan also advises Generation X to:

1. **See relationships in terms of what they have to offer, instead of what you want or need to get.** "Instead of asking to be introduced, offer someone the chance to introduce you. Instead of asking people to meet with each other, offer to bring people together," he says.

2. **Identify and seek out the right decision-makers.** List every decision that must be made to reach your goal and who will make that decision every step of the way. Those are the people you want to build a relationship with.

3. **Turn every new contact into a multiple contact.** While Generation X is a whiz at sending e-mails or leaving voice mails, Tulgan says that's not enough. Use those, and more (like an overnight mail package and personal visits)—all at the same time—when making a business contact. Be sure you have something to talk about once you do make contact.

    Any connection should offer to add value. Make concrete proposals by certain deadlines and then deliver.

4. **Keep your communications interesting and useful.** Clip articles you think might be intriguing to the person, and send with a personal note. Direct that person to your personal homepage, make a video presentation of yourself, research and write up an article detailing interesting facts the person would find helpful. Or, come up with a prototype of a new product you are inventing. Just remember to keep whatever you do in good taste.

5. **Retain the positive energy in the relationship.** Be trustworthy, a good listener, a motivator, a supporter, respectful and kind.

It's Not Your Workplace, Anymore

If you're say, over 36, guess what Generation X is saying about you?

"You just don't get it."

"You don't have a clue."

Insulted? You who went to see the Rolling Stones before they were grandfathers? You who discoed 'til dawn and drove the Beetle when it was around the first time? How can you not "get it?"

According to research, Baby Boomers (especially those in management) really don't understand the generation born between 1963 and 1977, and how work is done by them. Instead, older managers try to judge and manage younger workers based on their own life experiences. But let's face it: being a 28-year-old in 1999 is a whole different ball of wax than being a 28-year-old in 1979. The world is different for Generation X, and so is work.

So, then, must be managers.

Neil Stroul, is an organizational psychologist studying how Baby Boom managers deal with Generation X workers, and how conflicts between the two groups can be eased.

"It may sound cliché, but the answer is to be a good manager and use the opportunities that are already there to develop Generation X into the kind of workers that are wanted," Stroul says. "But Baby Boom managers are so focused on the work that they're losing the opportunities to engage Generation X."

Instead of focusing every conversation on work, managers should take time to understand what younger workers want from a job, and how the manager can help the employee attain that goal, Stroul says.

For example, Generation X wants to be self-reliant, and not slowly plod up the corporate ladder. Instead, these workers want to build a portfolio of skills, so a manager should focus on helping these employees see where they are now, where they want to be and how the company can aid the worker in building desired skills.

But that isn't happening, and the results are being felt throughout the workforce.

"Generation X feels de-personalized by managers because managers only want to talk about their work, and not about them as individuals. That makes them feel disposable, so they become more cynical and feel no loyalty to a company and have no problem leaving. All this just reinforces the stereotype of Generation X as not being able to stick to a job," Stroul says. "Generation X sees Baby Boomers as being dismissive to them."

Stroul says the key is remembering that Generation X has a work ethic, "it's just a different work ethic."

He says that there is "a real urgency" for Generation X and Boomers to have a better understanding of each other because of increasing conflicts on the job.

"I think there is a delayed maturation on both sides. With Generation X, you're really not dealing with young adults, but older adolescents. And now with Boomers, you're seeing people extend middle age and think of themselves as forever young. But they need to understand they can groom the next generation and not have to step aside," Stroul says.

He adds the key to ease the conflict is to remember that what is created now in the world and the workplace will benefit the generation that will enter the job market in the next millennium. And he adds that the criticisms of Generation X are not new—the G.I. generation had the same conflicts with Baby Boomers when they came on the scene.

Stroul says there are ways to open the lines of communications among the generations, and recommends a 10-pronged approach to easing conflict. Specifically, he advises:

1. **Learn to pass the torch.** "This would go much more smoothly if there was a spirit of generosity behind it from the Boomer managers," he says.

2. **Adjust to an information-rich environment.** "If you create a culture where people act as filters and pass on valuable information as they come across it, then you build a sense of community."

3. **Accumulate wisdom.** "Play to each other's strengths. Generation X is technologically savvy. But Boomers are corporate savvy."

4. **Build credibility and trustworthiness.** Generation X is often alienated from Boomers because older managers break promises, or take actions that force younger workers to question the motives of managers.

5. **Forge developmental alliances.** "It's very hard to predict the future. You cannot just manage performance, but must look at the development of workers," Stroul says.

6. **Remember that work is evolutionary.** "Boomers had the opportunity to transform the workplace, and Xers will have those same expectations."

7. **Appreciate and foster the need for independence.** "The greatest managers are those who disappear and the place runs fine," he says.

8. **Focus on community rather than loyalty.** When managers whine about job-hopping Xers, Stroul says, "Get over it." "If you want people to stay long term, then you're going to have to make them a member of the community. The more you do to foster work/life balance, the better it will be," he says.

9. **Find a common cause.** "Both Boomers and Xers should be thinking of the generation to come."

10. **Accept the new career paradigm.** "Don't have a pouting, resentful attitude about the new generation of workers. Let them spread their wings."

Bunny Slippers: An Optional Office Supply

Most of us these days have some kind of home office. Whether it's a fancy setup with all the latest technological gizmos or just a computer in the corner of a room, we like to call it the "office" or the "study." But wait ...

are those dirty sweat socks on your printer? And—could it possibly be—your research notes are being filed on the exercise bike?

One of the biggest problems with working at home is that we don't take the time and the effort to set up our workspace correctly. The result: an inefficient and stressful work environment—exactly what we had hoped to escape when we left the office!

So whether you work at home part time or full time, there are a few guidelines to make the whole process more productive and enjoyable:

- ☑ **A home office is not a personal dumping ground.** Unused exercise equipment, broken appliances and newspapers from 1992 should not be in the office. It is not a place for your kids to play. If you are serious about working at home, the office space is to be used for work. Period.

- ☑ **Discipline yourself.** This is the time to set up your own ground rules—you're not going to use office time to clean the house, work on your child's Halloween costume or search the Internet for the answers to baseball trivia questions. If you find yourself easily distracted by home activities, set aside a certain time of the day that you will take an hour to dabble in another interest. Set a timer, and return to work when it goes off.

- ☑ **Eliminate distractions.** When was the last time you got a lick of work done with kids around? True, some people have been able to run businesses while taking care of their children, but many will find the stress detrimental to productivity. Consider the work at hand and the age of your children. It may be beneficial to find at least part-time care for small children so you can work uninterrupted for a certain number of hours. Statistics have shown people are much more productive at home, so it probably will mean you need help for less time than if you were in a company environment.

- ☑ **Be dependable.** Nothing kills a business faster or makes a boss question a home arrangement more than if you can't be located. Setting office hours each day lets everyone know they can find you at certain times.

☑ **Be honest.** If you cannot find care for a young child—say an ear infection has kept him or her home from school—then tell clients up front that you may be interrupted. Let them know they may hear video games being played in the background by teenagers.

☑ **Set the boundaries.** It's not unusual when you start working at home for others to see it as an opportunity to spend more time with you or to expect you to perform baby-sitting or house-keeping duties. Let your friends, family and neighbors know that you are working and cannot "fill in" when they need a baby-sitter, or chat for a few hours each morning over a cup of coffee.

☑ **Be comfortable.** There's nothing worse than trying to work using a chair that doesn't fit and a desk that wobbles. You may not need $10,000 worth of new office equipment and furniture, but you certainly need to be comfortable in your space. Keep in mind that about 75 percent of the small busi-nesses started each year fail to last more than five years, ac-cording to the Small Business Administration. If you're un-sure what you need, consult with others who work from home or buy the bare minimum you think you'll need, and then build on later.

☑ **Have fun.** Working at home is kind of like playing hooky while everyone else is going to school. As long as it doesn't offend a client, decorate the office the way you want. Put your feet up on the desk and play your favorite music. Wear your fuzzy slippers if they make you think better. And smile when you hear traffic into town is backed up for two miles.

Little Miss Muffet Should Have Had A Dog

If you work from your home, either full or part time, you probably feel pretty lucky. You don't have to fight the traffic, you get to wear your bathrobe if you want and no co-worker is hitting you up to contribute money for another employee's baby shower.

Everything is pretty hunky-dory. In fact, you're so relaxed you haven't bothered to lock the doors, you don't hesitate to brag to everyone in the grocery store that you work from home and anyone can look in the window and see all your nice, expensive office equipment.

With that attitude, working from home could become your worst nightmare.

Just because you don't go into an office does not mean you are not vulnerable to thieves and others who want to take advantage of your lax attitude. In fact, just as car jacking gained in frequency after annoying car alarms made it easier to just grab the car with the person in it, home invasions may become more likely because burglars have to become more aggressive when people are at home working, says John Perkins, a self protection expert.

"Home invasion is extremely dangerous because once a criminal gets into your home or apartment he is now out of sight from easy detection and he could now do whatever he has in mind," Perkins says.

Perkins, a former New York City police detective who also has been an international bodyguard, says that it is naïve for people to believe rising violence in the workplace will not follow them home. Especially, he says, if your work involves contact with people who may have a reason to want to confront you personally—and that could mean in your home office, with your family nearby.

For that reason, Perkins advises a number of steps be taken by those working from home, to protect themselves and their families. Among them:

1. **Getting a dog.** In a fenced yard, the dog can provide good company for your children, as well as signal trouble outside. When inside, the dog can alert you to anyone near the house when you are working. If you must have clients in the house, have the dog trained to sit quietly in the same room.

2. **Securing the doors and windows.** In addition to keeping doors and windows locked at all times, get an intercom for the front or back doors. These inexpensive systems are easy to

install and allow you to listen for outside activity as well as inquire who is at a door without opening it. Also, use covered peepholes for solid doors. Uncovered peepholes allow anyone on the outside to look in the peephole and determine when you approach.

At the same time, use window blinds that lower from the top, so that you can still get light, but don't display expensive equipment to outsiders.

If you can afford it, a video system is the best for screening visitors. If not, a good perimeter alarm system—that is turned on while you are at home—is a good idea.

3. **Protecting your privacy.**

    There's no reason everyone has to know you work from home. In fact, the fewer people the better. Use a company name with a post office box, or some other delivery address other than your home. Use your company name in the phone book without the address listing, and answer the phone with your company name.

    Forget just putting your first initial with your last name in the phone book. Everyone knows this is a trick mostly used by women—a perfect tip-off to the bad guys. Have a male voice on your answering machine.

4. **Being aware.** You may be running around on company business, your mind on the work you have to do when you get home. That makes it easy for a criminal to follow you home. Make sure you check your rear view mirror when driving. If you suspect someone is following you, drive around the block. If you are suspicious, use your car phone to call police or drive to a well-lit place or police department.

5. **Covering the bases.** If you must have an associate or client come in your home on business, always have another appointment to keep—lunch with a spouse, another meeting, etc., so that they know someone will be checking up on you.

    Always meet someone for the first time in a public place. If it is a sales person, then call the company to confirm the person's identity, and try to get a physical description. Call your local Chamber of Commerce if you are not familiar with the business.

6. **Delivering the goods.** Overnight package deliveries and courier services probably will be a fact of life if you work from home, but anyone can put on a uniform and use a van to pose as a delivery person. If you are not familiar with the delivery service, do not open the door, but have the package placed on the step. Wait several hours before retrieving it—bad guys can hide in the bushes and grab you when the door opens.

   Only open the door to sign for a package if you are sure it is a legitimate service.

Beating the New Kid Blues

Nearly all of us can remember the first days of school and the attack of "new kid" nerves. But we also can recall that the anxiety slowly dissipated once someone patiently explained what all the ringing bells meant, showed us where the bathrooms were and introduced us to other kids who taught us to play kick ball at recess.

Then we grew up and got jobs. And found out pretty quickly that no one was likely to patiently teach us anything, help us understand procedures or show us the ropes—including the location of the nearest bathroom.

And yet, it's more critical than ever that we learn the ins and outs of a new job as soon as possible. Companies are intent on reacting quickly to changing global markets and competition, and that means that each worker must pick up the pace of learning a new job and become productive in a much shorter amount of time.

"First impressions are lasting impressions, and these days, those judgments about people happen pretty quickly. You don't have a lot of time to make your mark," says David Opton, a professional networking expert.

With a majority of workers liable to switch jobs as many as six times in a lifetime, the odds are pretty good that you'll be the new kid on the block sometime, whether it's your first job or your third. Opton says the key to success in any organization "is how things get done."

"There are formal and informal parts of an organization, and the key is to become a part of the informal group, because otherwise you might as well be isolated in lockup. And becoming part of this group is even more critical the higher you go in the company," he says.

Opton recommends that in order to have high impact in your first months on the job you should:

- ☑ **Ask questions.** Never assume anything. Show interest in who people are and what they do. Listen carefully.

- ☑ **Get it straight.** When you were hired, were expectations clearly outlined? Probably not. Define with your supervisor what is expected of you and how this relates to customers and co-workers. Set up a 90-day plan of what you want to achieve. Go over it with a supervisor to make sure it matches the company vision and mission. If you are a manager, share this commitment with your team so they understand your expectations and goals for yourself and for them.

- ☑ **Don't rush it.** If you're not sure what to do, don't try to bluff or bulldoze your way through. Those are the kinds of mistakes that can haunt you for a long time. Instead, ask for input and be collaborative when you can.

- ☑ **Continually keep in touch.** Just because you've come up with this plan doesn't mean it can't run into roadblocks. Talk to supervisors, subordinates and peers to make sure things are on track. Subtle adjustments can be made until you are fully accepted.

- ☑ **Gather information.** By chatting with others over morning coffee, having lunch or enjoying a walk after work with co-workers, you can learn about potential conflicts, different personalities and even learn who wanted the job you have. This can help you cross the minefield of office politics without getting into serious trouble your first few months on the job.

"In jobs today, it's rarely about competency," Opton says. "It's usually about fit."

He explains that if you fit with co-workers, the company culture and find a way to become a team member as early as possible, your chances of success are much greater.

"Of course you should feel good that you were hired for the job, but this is a two-way street. The company now feels that you must fulfill your part of the job, and that means you fitting in smoothly. You won the job competition, but that does not ensure that things will go your way all the time," Opton says.

Further, with more companies cutting training and development because of budget belt-tightening, Opton says it's more important than ever before that each person develop career skills.

"At any level, you have to remember that nobody cares as much about you as you do about yourself," he says. "Have skills will travel. It's not a bad philosophy."

Propeller Heads Have Feelings, Too

"To err is human, to really foul things up requires a computer."
—*Farmer's Almanac*

That bit of wisdom was written 20 years ago, but it unfortunately is still true today for many of us in the workplace who not only don't understand technology—we don't want to.

Unfortunately, it's not really a choice anymore. Because if companies want to survive—and employees want their careers to thrive—then they are going to have to "make nice" with computers and those who understand them.

But that may sound easier than it really is.

James Martin, a well-known business and technology guru, explains that the problem is not with the technology, but with those who must teach it and those who must learn it.

For example, Martin says that often the most stubborn employees who resist technology are none other than the top dogs—the CEOs. That results in a quagmire of communication problems between management and "propeller heads"—the technical professionals who create the systems and who themselves are not the most sociable beings.

"Many people who go into the computer industry are very uncomfortable talking to people—they go into the technical profession because they can tell a machine what to do and it will. They don't have to get along with a lot of people," Martin says.

So now it's clear that one group doesn't want to talk and one group doesn't want to listen. Stalemate?

Not necessarily. Martin says that "bridging people" should be found at every company. These employees would be "enterprise engineers" who would be able to understand the techies' language and then translate it into everyday terms so that upper management grasps it more easily and quickly sees the advantages.

"Technology is very important to companies these days, and the people in charge need to understand what these propeller heads are telling them," Martin says. "If the communication is not being made, then you've got a problem that escalates from just being a problem into something that's potentially catastrophic."

One of the keys to this whole communication process is understanding which business decisions should be left to a machine, and which should be handled by a human. He says that machines should handle[6] :

- ☑ **Straightforward choices,** such as when to reorder goods.

- ☑ **Complex but precise logic,** such as the allocation of gates to incoming flights at a large airport.

- ☑ **Logic so intricate that a human being cannot compete with a computer's capabilities,** such as the rescheduling of equipment after failures and delays on a major commercial airline.

- ☑ **Storing, recalling and applying vast amounts of data and rules.**

And those decisions best left to a human? Those include:

- ☑ **When sensitivities such as emotions or feelings or intuition predominate.**

- ☑ **When people need to be inspired or led.**

- ☑ **When required skills include drawing analogies,** associating diverse ideas or recognizing patterns familiar to humans, such as common behaviors and reactions.

- ☑ **When negotiations and protocol are demanded.**

NOTES

[1] Jim Harris, *Getting Employees to Fall in Love With Your Company* (Amacom, 1996)

[2] Matt Weinstein, *Managing to Have Fun* (Simon & Schuster, 1996)

[3] Dr. Rick Brinkman and Dr. Rick Kirschner, *Dealing With People You Can't Stand* (McGraw Hill, 1994)

[4] Pat Nickerson, *Managing Multiple Bosses* (Amacom, 1999)

[5] Bruce Tulgan, *Work This Way* (Hyperion, 1998)

[6] James Martin, *Cybercorp: The New Business Revolution* (Amacom, 1996)

3

CAREER PLANS

In the last 15 years, I have moved 10 times. Some of those moves have been within 20 miles, others have been across the country. Some I made while single, some while newly married, others I made with a newborn in my arms or two kids in tow.

Moving that much is not something I planned, although I always had a great desire to see more of the world—I just thought I'd do it sight-seeing, not moving.

With this many moves under my belt, you'd think I'd become quite adept at reading local maps, finding my way around quickly. And that's partly true. I usually do get my bearings fairly quickly in a new environment. I just don't do it with a map.

When I got married, my husband became quite concerned that I started out for anywhere without first studying a map. My continued lack of interest in the large atlas he put in my car finally prompted him to draw maps of a smaller area when we moved to a new city. He'd pinpoint where we were, where the bank was located, the grocery store, a video place, etc.

This seemed somehow better than that big map, I thought, and accepted his hand-drawn maps with the arrows saying "you are here." But the problem was, once I started driving, I was no longer "here." It became, well, "there," and there was no "there" on the map. I'd drive around and around, becoming more lost, consulting the little map more frequently. When I finally found my way back home (usually after stopping to ask directions), my husband would be totally exasperated, as only husbands can be.

"How could you get lost?" he would say. "You had a map!"

"Yes," I would agree. "But how am I supposed to use a map to find my way when I'm lost? I don't know where I am on that little map, so how do I know where to go?"

I don't think this issue bothered me nearly as much as it did him. I use the method of location I have always used. I find landmarks and implant them in my mind. I use those as reference points, then always make sure my car has a full tank of gas. Maybe the routes to my destinations are not always straight, but I always get there. And once I do, I never forget how to get there again.

Unfortunately, this method of becoming familiar with a new place has not been appreciated by my children, either. Before my two sons were born, I could get lost in peace. Now, I hear from the backseat, "Mom, I'm getting carsick. All this twisting and turning is making me sick! We're lost!"

"I'm not really lost, and we've turned around less than a dozen times," I'll say. "Just enjoy the scenery!"

"Mooommmm...I've seen that building three times already! You keep driving past it! Look at Dad's map, Mom!"

So, again you may be wondering about the point of my story. It's that some people have career paths that sort of imitate my wanderings. They know basically where they want to go, they just don't have a map and they sure don't know how to read one. They just become more lost. Unlike me, however, they cannot turn around and around until they get it right.

It's a sad but true fact that many people reach their mid-40s before they realize they're lost. They're on the road to nowhere with their career, and they don't have a clue where they took a wrong turn. Or, young people get turned around, but don't know enough to stop and ask directions from someone who might be familiar with the territory.

This chapter looks at what you can do to make your career path a little smoother, a little more focused and improve the chances that you won't lose your way.

A Pocketful of Business Cards, and Other Miracles

Networking.

For some, this word provokes images of the irritating louse at your sister's wedding who tried to put a hard sell on you about some miracle product and kept shoving his card in your hand.

Or, you may believe networking is something that only high-powered professionals do—and do well. It's not for the average worker who may never see the corporate office with a window or be considered on a fast track to success.

But networking is really a simple process, one that can be beneficial to anyone in any kind of career situation. Because networking is simply a way to build relationships and learn to be helpful to other people.

"I like to compare networking with the old barn-raising parties where people came together and combined their skills and talents to get a job done in one day that would have otherwise taken one person much longer," says Donna Fisher, a networking expert.

Fisher says that networking has gotten a bad rap from networking "mongrels" who are in your face, pushing the hard sell and being nuisances.

"Our society tends to want immediate gratification, and you get people trying to oversell you. The true spirit of networking is one that has a much broader, more relaxed approach," she says.

Fisher stresses that the aim of networking is to give and to get information and to establish relationships with a variety of people. Effective networking means a contact might not pay off for years, but one day you need some crucial information, and presto! There's the name and phone number in your Rolodex.

A key point to networking is to remember that you're not "bothering" someone when you ask questions. Fisher says when you let someone know you are looking for a referral, prospect or service provider, you are giving that person information. You should focus on distributing the information to enough people so that you can reach your goal and get the support or contact you want.

Here are some ideas to get you on the road to terrific networking:[1]

☑ **List five major accomplishments** you are proud of in your life. This gives you information about who you are as a networker and what type of resources you can offer others.

☑ **Give up the lone ranger mentality.** Don't think you know it all, are the best and never need help. You don't, you're not, and yes, you do.

☑ **Make a diagram of your network.** Write your name in the middle, then draw lines for the major spokes of your network (family, business associates, clubs, church, alumni, etc.) This diagram will show the magnitude and diversity of your network.

☑ **Introduce yourself in a clear, concise and personable way that generates interest.** When someone asks what you do, don't just say, "I'm a franchise consultant." Try something like, "I help small companies become large companies through franchising."

☑ **Be gracious and courteous with everyone.** The biggest mistake is burning bridges by being rude or short-tempered with a person who might be useful in the future. Send a thank-you note after an event, ask how you can assist a host or simply hold the elevator door.

☑ **Business cards.** These should be attractive and representative of what you do. Have enough to pass out appropriately.

☑ **Nurture the network.** Every week, call at least one person you have not talked to in at least 90 days.

☑ **Return calls within 24 hours.**

☑ **Find opportunities to ask, "Who do you know who...?"** Be explicit about what type of person you want to contact.

Get a Ladder and Climb Out of That Career Pit

One of the most difficult things to realize about yourself may be that you're stuck in a rut. A career rut. Doing the same thing year after year, for the same company, for the same boss, with little thought to your future.

The safety of a steady paycheck, a comfortable job that yields decent benefits and a bearable amount of aggravation can lull you into complacency about your career.

Big mistake.

Why? Because you may be depriving yourself of challenging, interesting, rewarding work by simply letting your career "happen" to you, rather than actively seeking ways to make it something you enjoy and want to do.

This does not necessarily mean you need to jump ship and plunge into a new field willy-nilly, with only the thought of breaking the mold. It may simply be that you need to look around your own environment and see what's up. Is there something you would rather be doing within your company? A position you covet but have done nothing to attain? Have you become a part of the woodwork so that interesting projects are not offered to you? If so, take heart. Things can change—and you're just the one to make those changes.

Richard Koonce, who offers advice on career planning and coaching, says American workers need to learn to "work smart."

"People need to ask themselves if they feel stuck," Koonce says. "They need to consider what they are doing to explore other options. What I see—particularly with people who have been with an organization for a long time—is docility. People often feel the company is going to take care of them."

He says if a person is suffering in silence and is unhappy with a position or career path then "get out of the victim mode."

Instead, take stock of your skills and talents, and decide what you would like to do. Then, visit the boss.

"Get out of the mindset that if the employer wanted you to do that, then he would have asked you," Koonce says. "Go see your boss and ask them for ideas or a strategy to help assist you in your career development."

And while some supervisors may be ill equipped to offer such advice, they may be able to refer you to someone else within your company or provide names of outside help. If not, begin the search process yourself.

Consider someone you work with or someone in another department whose opinion you value, or approach a friend or acquaintance or business associate who may be able to help you plot a new course.

The key: Start talking. Network with others to let them know what you want, and what's important to you. Brainstorm with others for ideas and develop a plan and a strategy. Make inquiries about jobs or companies you are interested in, to make sure reality fits your expectations.

"Look before you leap," Koonce cautions. "Interview a prospective boss as they interview you."

Another common mistake is that some workers fail to step back and truly assess whether they have chosen the correct field for themselves. For example, a salesman may think he just dislikes the company he works for and simply switch to another company and keep doing the thing he hates—selling.

By performing a career self-evaluation, you can look to see what really interests you, and whether your current positions meets those desires.

"Jobs can be like relationships," he says. "Job hopping in rapid succession is like hopping from one love affair to another. There's no real satisfaction."

One way to avoid career ruts is by getting exposure to a wide variety of experiences the first 10 years of a career. For example, try a few years in the private sector, a few in the government arena and a few at a nonprofit organization.

"What you're really after early on is breadth of experience, and adding depth later," Koonce says. "This can give you latitude and flexibility."

Koonce also offers these tips:[2]

☑ **Don't hide behind your desk.** Develop a sense of where the organization is going. Identify key players.

☑ **Become an industry watcher and tracker.**

☑ **Assess prospects for promotion where you are now.**

☑ **Determine whether your work style and values match those of your employer.**

☑ **Ask yourself if your employer is committed to developing you.** Are there training programs, tuition reimbursements, job rotations or task force assignments?

☑ **Learn to spot the warning signs that indicate your job is in trouble,** such as ruthless budget-slashing, poor performance reviews, etc.

———◆———

Delegate Tasks, Not Chaos

Much of the career advice these days has to do with learning to delegate. You cannot do it all yourself, the experts say, so you must let others help you out.

But that may be easier said that done. First, you may not feel comfortable delegating. After all, no one can do a particular task as well you can, and second, it's just easier to do it yourself rather than having to explain it to someone else then having to watch over them every second.

And that's why you are swamped with work, constantly stressed and always under deadline pressure. Because if you take that attitude about giving others responsibilities, then you're part of the problem.

James R. Lucas has written and lectured about leadership. He says that many people do not delegate tasks, "but delegate confusion."

"Many people look at delegating tasks they hate, or delegating things they don't really think about or care about," he says. "We're kidding ourselves if we think that we can direct people to a task if we don't have a clear vision of what needs to be done."

He says that delegating is really on-the-job training, providing those in an organization a chance to stretch and grow. And if someone can't delegate, then they're actually hurting the business because it undermines trust and motivation among employees.

"Control is a major issue for every human being, and many people have a personal insecurity about delegating. They may think that someone else will do a better job than them, and that they'll lose their jobs," Lucas says. "But that's a false fear. Because those who fear it the most are the most dispensable because they are not growing and taking chances."

Still, there are some guidelines to follow when delegating to make sure it is a win-win situation for everyone. Lucas suggests that delegation should include:

☑ **A clear vision.** When you decide to delegate, know what needs to be done, what the outcome should be and who can best do the task. Define clearly to yourself why this job can be delegated, and how it relates to your work and to the organization.

☑ **Making it positive.** When delegating, it should not be a negative to you or to the person receiving the task. Outline the job for the person, then ask for them to think about what it will take to get the job done, what resources will be needed, the amount of time required. Then ask the person to return to you with their thoughts, and any questions.

"The best delegations are negotiations," Lucas says. "When they come back with questions, there may be something you have not thought of, or it may let you know that this person doesn't have enough knowledge to do the task."

He adds that by encouraging this exchange, you have established "that you don't think the person is stupid if they have questions."

☑ **Getting it straight.** Once you have established the delegation, then ask the person to repeat the assignment back to you, or even better, get it in writing. This gives everyone a clear idea of what needs to be done, and when.

☑ **Following up.** There's nothing worse than giving an assignment, then hovering over that person's desk, bugging them daily about what they're doing and why. Once you delegate, back off. Keep track of what is going on through scheduled meetings, but if you see that this person is keeping you informed of progress, is on track and handling the project well, then "you can loosen the reins," Lucas says.

☑ **Not panicking:** if there is a glitch, don't yank the project away and dive in. Instead, write the person a note outlining the problem, and give a date for when issue should be resolved. Then, if the deadline approaches and the problem still exists, you can step in. If it's been handled, then there's no reason to interfere.

☑ **Forgetting the clone idea.** There is only one you, and that's why you delegate in the first place, isn't it? So don't expect someone else to handle a job exactly the way you would.

"No one will ever be ready if you wait for them to be ready," Lucas says. "If a person looks 50 percent qualified, then give them a chance to grow another 50 percent. You want to stretch people, not stress them. You don't train drones."

────◆──◆──◆────

Mentors Provide Savvy Advice

Planning a career strategy is tricky business. One misstep and you could miss the opportunity of a lifetime. Choosing one wrong road could set you back for years in reaching your goal. If we had a crystal ball, we think, it would all be much easier.

Well, there is a crystal ball of sorts. It's called mentoring.

Mentors can be people inside or outside your company, but the role is the same: to give you the benefit of their knowledge and experience so you make the right decisions for your career.

How do you find a mentor, and how do you get one to take on the challenge? And, more importantly, how do you make sure you don't get a dud who dead ends your career with lousy advice?

Cynthia Berryman-Fink, a consultant and trainer, says most solid mentor relationships evolve naturally, either through friendships at work or through private contacts.

"The key is that you have to find someone who is successful in their career and who also wants to teach or coach," she says. "But it can seem really artificial if you just walk up and ask someone to be your mentor. They must get something out of the relationship also."

Specifically, you must heed the advice of the mentor and not become a pain in the backside. The mentor is not someone who solves all your problems, but someone who helps you over rough spots (such as office politics) and helps you plan and execute projects that upper management will appreciate.

And because that person might be privy to inside information that is shared with you, it is crucial you not violate that trust by blabbing to others what you have learned. Much of what you gain from a mentoring relationship comes from watching and listening to how more-experienced people handle workplace issues. The key is your willingness to work hard and make the relationship worthwhile to the mentor because of your enthusiasm and commitment.

If you decide that a mentor might help your career, then here are some issues to consider:

☑ **A good mentor is someone who has a solid reputation in your field or within your company.** Flashy performers might look good in the short run, but they could burn out early and take you with them. Look for those who have earned respect from managers and employees over the years.

☑ It is often beneficial to **have a mentor who not only has good contacts within the company, but a solid relationship with others in the community.** Such networking skills are the name of the game these days. Sometimes those who are within a few years of retiring are interested in becoming mentors as a way of leaving something of themselves behind.

☑ When considering a possible mentor, **take the time to sit down and outline your goals and how this person's specific skills will help you meet those challenges.** Would you feel comfortable confiding in this person? Are your values similar?

☑ **Use caution in cross-gender mentor relationships.** "Mentoring relationships between men and women are often looked upon negatively by observers," Berryman-Fink says. "They can be viewed very suspiciously. Be very careful."

☑ **Be willing to take honest feedback.** The mentor will certainly give you pats on the back when deserved, but you also should be willing to take negative comments as well. There might be some snotty comments from co-workers who are jealous of your relationship with your mentor. Simply acknowledge the relationship and then go on with your work. Gloating is not allowed. While you should meet with your mentor frequently, try to keep the sessions discreet.

☑ The mentor might be able to help you out in the office by possibly recommending you for certain projects or mentioning your hard work and abilities within the organization. But **it is not appropriate to publicize your relationship with the mentor as a way to garner more attention for yourself.**

———————◆———————

The Better Mouse Trap...As Seen on TV

When we think of entrepreneurs, we often think of people like Henry Ford or Bill Gates, those who came up with brilliant ideas that changed world events and made them very, very rich.

Not us, we think. We've got a mortgage, car payments, kids. Striking out on our own isn't for us. It's for risk-takers who are so talented and so smart they can make anything successful.

Hah.

Entrepreneurs are often just ordinary people who have the desire and the skills to make an idea work, says one expert.

"These people have a vision and a goal and they take a systematic approach to making it happen—whether it's designing a new clothespin or a really good electric car or simply by offering innovative services," says Jim Lang, an entrepreneurial expert and lecturer.

Still, Lang cautions that budding entrepreneurs often make a fatal mistake: they believe that their idea is going to make them a ton of money overnight.

"There is the assumption that an entrepreneur can get rich quickly—and is usually tied to that 'great idea'," Lang says. "They think all they have to do is dream it up and the money will flow."

Successful entrepreneurs, he says, minimize risk by carefully planning their business strategy and doing the research necessary to know if a plan will work.

Lang offers some advice for those considering striking out on their own:[3]

☑ **Assess your current skills.** Are you an expert at hanging dry-wall, or designing software? Look at what you can and cannot do and determine how you learned your skills. While you will certainly need fundamental skills such as financial management, marketing and team building, you need to be honest about your area of expertise—and what help you will need from others.

☑ **You can't do it all by yourself.** Lang advises being wary of "the relative who does a little accounting." Better to find the best people for the job. Ask other entrepreneurs for recommendations. Network with friends, relatives and associates to get their feedback.

☑ **Communicate effectively.** If you can't make others listen to you, your idea is going to wither on the vine. Put yourself in the other person's shoes and think about what's in it for her. Make a good first impression by being professional, organized and well prepared. Adapt your presentation to the person—listen and take your cues from her.

☑ **Never miss an opportunity to learn.** Check into local colleges or universities or community classes that can help you expand your business savvy. Never doubt the importance of improving your research, and use all resources.

☑ **Get organized.** Develop a healthy respect for the bottom line and be realistic when looking at profits and losses. Take a course in financial management or get yourself a good accountant.

☑ **Set positive goals.** Be realistic and don't overreach.

Remember that becoming your own boss is not without problems. Entrepreneurs often drive themselves quite hard, and the quest for the next job or next project blocks everything else out of their lives. Lang cautions that before deciding to become an entrepreneur, sit down with family and friends and outline your goals. Ask them to tell you when you're becoming too stressed out—and then listen to them when they tell you.

"The adrenaline kicks in and keeps going and going," Lang says. "You need someone who can haul you back. Stress in the end is the silent killer for entrepreneurs. Think about other people who take holidays; you can, too. The business will still be there when you get back."

———•—————

Nosebleeds At the Top

You've worked hard, put in long hours, always done your best and more—and now you're about to reap the rewards of a job well done. You're going to the head of the class. You're going to be a supervisor.

After the initial jubilation and congratulations, a funny feeling stirs in the pit of your stomach. Then it heads for your toes, turning your knees to jelly. Your head starts to pound.

That's when it hits you: you're so nervous it's a wonder your teeth don't chatter. What do you know about being the boss? How will you know what to do and when? What if your employees hate you? How can you begin ordering your friends to do what you say?

Being a first-time supervisor is no cakewalk, but keep in mind that you wouldn't be in that position if you didn't deserve it. You're obviously intelligent and capable, and those two qualities will take you far. Still, there are stumbling blocks to your success. Bob Nelson, a motivation and incentive management expert, says that new managers must first understand that they will need new skills and priorities when they assume their new positions. Instead of doing a job well themselves, they will be coaching others on how to do it the right way, he says.

"Don't make the mistake of telling employees to get out of your way while you fix it for them," Nelson says. "After a while, your employees will think they can't do anything right."

Jim Miller, a successful businessman and creator of the "Best Boss/ Worst Boss" contest, agrees.

"The one thing I hear over and over is that people need to be told (by managers) how important they are—that bosses really care about them," Miller says. "And remember to always say thank you to your employees."

Another key to avoiding future problems is to determine ahead of time what you hope to accomplish and how this aligns with a company's goals and missions. By meeting with your supervisor, you can outline your agenda and make adjustments as needed.

Many companies offer new manager training that will help to ease the butterflies in your stomach and provide you with the knowledge to get off on the right foot. Still, it doesn't hurt to have a little sage advice from two management pros, Nelson and Miller. Their advice for new managers includes:

- ☑ On the first day, **call everyone together and outline your ideas and philosophies.** Bring coffee and doughnuts and make it an informal chat.

  Remember: your success is dependent on others—so be respectful of the other talent in the room. "Spend time with each person and find out what they're doing and get their ideas on where they think things should be going," Nelson says.

  If you are in the uncomfortable position of having been promoted from within and beating out a co-worker or friend for the job, you should immediately address the issue. Find out if your new position is going to cause problems and if so, what you can do to address those issues.

- ☑ **Keep communication open.** Stress how you are open to the opinions and ideas of others and then follow through. Miller urges managers to "listen to employees, be flexible and respond to anything they have to say."

- ☑ **Learn to delegate.** Nelson points out your employer is paying you a manager's pay so you will manage—not be a programmer, accounting clerk or customer service representative. Focus on results—not how those results are achieved.

- ☑ **Manage thyself.** Now that you've got the job, don't think you can "wing it." Take some management courses at local colleges, stay up on industry news through magazines and newsletters and network with other professionals.

Miller's final advice: "Be yourself. Don't try to be something you're not. Then you'll be successful."

Ain't Nobody As Good As I Is

You've spent hours on your resume, proofing it for typos and honing it until it gleams with professionalism and oozes talent. You slip it into the envelope, confident an employer will read it and beg you to work for the company.

Now how about that cover letter? Did you craft it as carefully? Did you even send one?

If you didn't, don't count on that begging to start soon—or for the employer to even read that sterling resume you sweated buckets over. Because without a cover letter, that resume may be headed for the recycling bin.

"People don't realize how important a cover letter is," says Robbie Miller Kaplan, a career consultant. "In the letter, you've got to grab their attention and tell them what you can do for them. You need to tell them how you can meet the job requirements."

At the same time, Kaplan says that those who do remember to send a cover letter often goof it up. By starting out with "I" and then continuing to sound very self-serving is a quick way to have your resume tossed out. The most important thing, she says, it to convey how you can do the job.

How? By doing your homework so that you sound well informed about the job, the industry, the work environment and who is doing the hiring. Another key: "Sound like you wrote it just for me even if you've sent hundreds of others out just like it," Kaplan says.

Some other cover letter tips:[4]

- ☑ **Forget the bizarre paper.** You want your cover letter easy to read and easy to photocopy.

- ☑ **If you're overqualified, downplay it a bit in the cover letter.** Tell them what you want them to know.

- ☑ **Be honest, but don't sound desperate.** No matter how qualified you are, that whining sound will turn off an employer.

- ☑ **Use the letter to provide additional information that makes you sound right for the job.** For example, maybe you have volunteered for several conservation programs in your area and have a great passion for the subject—a fact that would be intriguing to an environmental company. Or, if you've had a really positive experience with a product produced by a potential employer, let them know in your letter.

☑ **Make your opening paragraph strong.** Try beginning with a question such as, "Could your organization use…If so, consider me for…"

☑ **Type all letters,** use single spacing for the text and double spacing between paragraphs.

☑ **Address each letter to a specific individual and include his or her name and job title in the inside address.** If you are sending an unsolicited letter, go to the local library or consult business listings to determine to whom it should go. Then call the company and double-check the name, title and spelling.

☑ **If you don't know what courtesy title a woman prefers, use "Ms."** If you are unable to determine the individual's gender, omit the courtesy title and begin with something like "Dear Kelley Smith" or "Kelley Smith."

☑ **Date the letter, sign it and include your phone number.**

☑ **No typos.** No grammatical errors. No attempts at humor. Be professional and be polite.

☑ **Be sure to follow up with a telephone call in a few days** to make sure the information was received, and to ask to discuss your qualifications in person. Don't be overbearing and make a pest of yourself. Managers are busy people and you could get on the reject list simply by not knowing when to hang up.

Don't Get Blasted with On-Line Resumes

As we all become more familiar with the world of cyberspace, we are more enamored with what the Internet can offer us: on-line shopping, cheaper travel services and endless access to information about nearly anything.

Of course, searching for a job on-line also has become more common. But if you're sending your resume into cyberspace, there is just one thing you need to know: Sender beware.

"There are some big time wolves out there," warns Pam Dixon, an on-line job search expert. "You run a lot of risks when you send your resume on-line."

Specifically, Dixon says that once you send that resume, it's very likely you will receive a message from one or more resume distribution services who will then hit you up for a fee ($50 to $100) to send your resume out "to thousands of recruiters."

"Job searchers should never have to pay to send their resume," Dixon says. "You can send that resume to thousands of people for free yourself."

For example, a resume can be sent to 7,000 recruiters for free by using Recruiters OnLine Network (recruitersonline.com), including 73 specialty categories, or to recruiters in specific parts of the country.

Still, Dixon advises that even though you can "blast" your resume to thousands, does not mean you should do so. In fact, Dixon says it is better to do your homework and choose sites that are "password protected" such as the On-line Career Center and E-Span.

"If you put your resume on-line with Yahoo! or UseNet for example, then it's open to everyone. It's going to get passed around on-line, and there are people who do nothing but find resumes and then post them on databases everywhere," she says. "Some people like that idea, but if you don't, then only go to databases that offer confidentiality and protection."

What could happen if your confidentiality is not protected? Dixon says there are companies that employ "salvagers"—human resources folks who search the Internet looking for resumes posted by current employees.

"Then they bring you in and try to 'salvage' you. They try and find ways to keep you from leaving the company," she says. "I know of at least seven Fortune 1000 companies that do this."

If you want to post your resume on-line, there are several tips that can not only make the process easier, but provide better results. Dixon advises:

☑ **Never provide references.** Recruiters often will call your references about job openings, not you. "It's a cheap psychological trick, but many believe that if you come to us, we don't want you," she says.

☑ **Use key words in your resume.** There are resume tracking databases that just hold your resume until a job comes open. Then this software searches for key words in a resume.

   "You need to be up on the language in your industry. Go to the job databases and find out what kinds of words they are using. You need to use as many of those as possible in your resume," she says.

☑ **Look for niche markets.** Dixon's favorite site is Attorney@Work because it does such a good job of breaking job searches into different categories. Look for sites that can offer you contacts in the field or industry that interests you.

When writing your on-line resume, you should study others that have been posted on-line in your field. For example, some do not use "career objectives," while others will require it. If you decide to use such an introduction, be specific, Dixon says.[5]

(Don't just say you want to "teach school," but that you want "to teach fourth grade in a self-contained classroom full time.")

An introductory paragraph becomes critical if you avoid the career objectives statement, and must highlight your "skills sets"—words that describe exactly what is special about you—and what employers usually search for in resume databases.

And don't worry about keeping your resume to one page. If you're a professional with years of experience, write tight and to the point—but make sure you include all your achievements and experience that would be of value to an employer, Dixon says.

With the growing interest in searching for jobs on-line, Dixon says it's a mistake to let golden opportunities on-line pass you by. Instead, she counsels that by doing your homework, you can learn how to post a winning resume that will land you the contacts you desire.

Move to the Top

When mapping out your career strategy, it might be a good idea to pull out a map—literally—to see what it has to offer. Because experts say that your willingness to relocate to a different part of the country—or the world—may determine your rate of success in a chosen field.

Jim Anderson, a relocation consultant, says that relocation "can make or break a career."

"Moving can be very important," he says. "The more you change jobs with different companies, the more you add to your inventory of skills. And if you're willing to move internationally, that can get you even further ahead in a company."

And while the number of people relocating for new jobs has not changed that much in the last several years, Anderson notes that the reason for those moves has altered.

"It used to be that a company told you to move to a new place, and you could take it or leave it. But you weren't going to have a job if you didn't go," he says. "Now, people are moving to enhance their careers."

Still, some employees are unwilling to relocate, no matter what it might cost a career, Anderson says.

"Many people will say it's because they don't want to move somewhere because of the high cost of living, but to be honest, I think that's just a way of saying they have personal reasons they don't want to move," he says. "It's just easier to tell the boss that. Most of the time people don't want to move because of family considerations."

Surveys show that two-thirds of those who relocate are between the ages of 35-45, and 65 percent have two or more children. Some 21 percent are under age 35.

"I think we have a much more mobile workforce these days," Anderson says. "We have cities growing and attracting workers all over the world."

At the same time, deciding to relocate is a tough decision, whether it affects an entire family or just a single worker. But with some careful considerations, experts say you can make the right decision for your career and your personal life. Among the issues to look at:

☑ **Income.** If you move, but your spouse cannot find a job in a new location, it could adversely affect your finances. Many recruiters are willing to help spouses find new jobs, so ask about a program. At the same time, a new job can significantly boost your income, perhaps in a way that will give your spouse some breathing room in finding a new position in a new city. Ask about signing bonuses and relocation packages before committing to a move.

☑ **Advancement.** Is this move critical to moving you toward your desired goal, perhaps at a faster rate than if you stayed put? Does it open new doors and provide new opportunities for learning? Are there people at the new company who would be willing to provide that boost to your career?

☑ **Family.** Many times it's understood that a family with a teen will not be willing to move, but it's not unheard of. All members of the family should be consulted about their feelings, and what the move would mean to them now and in the future.

☑ **Be open.** Always be willing to go on an interview and check out what the company—and new location—have to offer. Even if this job doesn't pan out, it can lead to contacts they may provide just the opportunity you seek in an area you desire.

☑ **Get the facts.** When reviewing a new location, it's possible to learn a great deal without ever leaving home. An Internet site, www.homefair.com, provides a look into everything from schools to churches to shopping to housing prices. If you get a chance to go for an interview, take a camera and shoot various pictures of the city. This gives you a chance to refresh your memory at a later date, and gives your family something to see, other than just facts and figures.

☑ **Value your decisions.** Maybe you do want to climb the corporate ladder, but don't want to move in order to do it. That's okay. Look for new opportunities within your company, and express a willingness to learn new skills. These can also charge your career, and may make you more comfortable in the long run.

NOTES

[1] Donna Fisher & Sandy Vilas, *Power Networking* (MountainHarbour, 1992)
[2] Dean Koonce, *Career Power* (Amacom, 1994)
[3] Jim Lang, *Make Your Own Breaks* (DBM, 1994)
[4] Robbie Miller Kaplan, *Sure-Hire Cover Letters* (Amacom, 1994)
[5] Pam Dixon & Sylvia Tierston, *How to Be Your Own Headhunter On-line* (Random House, 1995)

4

WORK GONE WRONG

I've already clued you in on my first job experience. It was an inauspicious beginning: I survived, just as I would survive all the rocky work experiences to follow.

Consider, for example, the job I held as a reporter covering Capitol Hill in Washington, D.C. One day, the boss called me into her office to complain about my work. Only one problem: she couldn't give me one example of my so-called poor performance. She rambled on for about 30 minutes, and when I left, I was confused and upset. Not 20 minutes later she called me into the conference room, where a stack of articles I had written for the last several months were on the table in front of her.

"You know," she says, "God sent me in here. I now see, by looking at your work, that you've done three times as much work as anyone in this office, and it's really very good. I guess God wanted to show me I was wrong."

Stunned, I didn't say a word. I simply went to my desk, pulled my resume from a drawer and made several copies of it on my lunch hour. I decided I couldn't always depend on divine intervention to help my career. I began sending out resumes to other news organizations that day, and landed another job within months. Hallelujah.

Since that time I've had some terrific jobs where my efforts were actually appreciated and rewarded. But, like millions of other people, I've had some work experiences I would just as soon forget, including:

➡ A large metropolitan newspaper contacted me for an interview after I sent a resume. In the middle of July, I took a bus, a subway, and walked five blocks in three-inch heels and a suit to arrive on time for my interview. The editor's first words: "We don't have a job for you. I just wondered what a girl from Oklahoma thought she was doing applying for a job here."

➡ I worked in an office with a man who was known for being a jerk. He threatened male employees, leered at females and generally made everyone miserable. Management tried to ignore him. One day, after a particularly offensive remark he made to the office in general, I simply turned to him and quietly told him to "shut up." Not a smart thing on my part, but a minute later I found myself being pursued by this man who was yelling obscenities as me. The faster I walked, the faster he came after me. Then I broke into a trot, weaving in and out of cubicles while gaping co-workers looked on. Now chasing me in earnest, the man and I whipped by the supervisor's office a couple of times before she finally got off the phone to see what was up. Her solution: a reprimand not to run in the office. To top it off, the high-speed pursuit made me late leaving work and I missed my bus.

➡ While covering a speech by a public official, another journalist from a television station approached me, telling me how "fine" I looked. I ignored him, until he began stroking my neck, in front of about 50 other people. My faced burned with humiliation, but I was young, inexperienced and didn't want to make a scene. When I got back to the office, I finally confided in another reporter what had happened. The result was that my managing editor officially lodged a complaint against the television journalist, who was promptly put on probation.

But that wasn't the only such incident: one time my doorbell rang at 2 a.m., and I found an intoxicated supervisor on my front step asking me if I wanted to have an affair. "No, thanks," I said, slamming the door in his face.

My point is that not all work experiences are enjoyable. Some are downright miserable, and often it's bad enough to cause physical and emotional problems. But there are places to get help—either from friends, family or professionals trained to deal with workplace issues. The key is remembering that you are not alone. Being unhappy at work happens to every-one sooner or later, but it does not have to be a permanent condition.

For Heaven's Sake, Get Out of Your Own Way

You've been passed up for that promotion—again. Your idea or project was rejected without discussion—again. You're with a third employer in as many years, and you've not received any kind of recognition for your work.

If this sounds familiar, it could be that the people you work for are just untalented, short-sighted twerps. But chances are that if your failure to thrive in a job is a familiar scenario, then it's time you looked in the mirror.

Because according to one expert, at least a quarter of the workforce is busy shooting itself out of the career saddle. In fact, Andrew J. DuBrin, a clinical psychologist and professor of management, says that career stupidity is so universal that it is committed by both young and old workers.

"A lot of people think that career management is using your common sense, or going to college and getting a degree," DuBrin says. "This other stuff just bounces off them. They just don't get it."

DuBrin says that while all of us trip "once or twice" in our careers, it is those people who chronically make the same mistakes who are destined to fail in attaining their career management goals. Think you're guilty? Consider these clear-cut forms of self-sabotage outlined by DuBrin:[1]

1. **Procrastination.** This may start in college by never completing assignments or by turning work in after a deadline. The pattern continues into the workplace, where such habits cause missed opportunities and irritate the boss.

2. **Deception and lying.** While some of us may stretch the truth from time to time to make ourselves look good, you know you've stepped over the line when you start taking full credit for someone else's work. Or, if you would be embarrassed if your version of the facts became public then you know you've gone too far.

3. **Stealing and pilfering.** Don't. Ever.

4. **Unprofessional image.** While dressing for success is important, it's also critical that your demeanor be suitable. You can be seen as unprofessional by being frivolous about serious situations; using youthful slang or expressions; or by being angry or cynical with others.

5. **Absenteeism or lateness.** This is the leading cause of employees being disciplined.

6. **Being self-righteous.** While ethics are certainly important, being totally inflexible does not show a tolerance for others. In this instance, try to list your problem areas, and see if you can modify some of your positions in order to get along better with others.

7. **Insensitivity.** Being abrasive and intimidating will get you yanked off the management track very quickly. While there are exceptions, eventually the bullies fall because no one is willing to help them when times get tough.

8. **Confronting the powerful.** By crossing swords with a more powerful person and venting your anger, you may just kiss your career good-bye. If you've got to get it out, write a nasty memo to the person, then tear it up. Or, discuss the problem with key personnel, tactfully and diplomatically.

If you're still unsure whether you're defeating yourself, ask co-workers or former bosses for an honest assessment of your performance. Question whether they believe you exhibit any habits that may derail your career.

Making Nice After You've Stomped Everyone's Toes

Most people can relate a few stories about some obnoxious co-worker who drove everyone nuts and had people plotting about how to get him fired. But what if it's you that co-workers can't stand—and you know it and want to change?

Well, first you must realize that it isn't going to be easy. Whatever overbearing, anti-social and grating behavior put you at the top of the workplace "most disliked" list won't be erased immediately. But it can be done, and if it is accomplished successfully, you and your co-workers will benefit greatly.

Daniel S. Hanson, a management expert, has had many opportunities to see such conflicts on the job. He says that if you want to turn things around, then you've got to map out a strategy that will involve regaining trust of co-workers and proving you are sincere.

In other words, let go of the macho job strategy that says you can't have friends at work (you can), and the idea that you don't need anyone but yourself for success (you do).

"That can be very cleansing when you decide to clear all that out and make some changes," Hanson says.

One of the first steps is to find someone you can trust to help you regain the ground you've lost. While it may be difficult to find a close co-worker to help you, consider someone from human resources or an ombudsman who can discreetly help you test the waters. This person can get a true indication of where your mistakes have been made, and what you need to do to correct them.

Also, it's important that a supervisor be assured of your sincere efforts to mend fences. Then, you must begin changing your ways, showing others in the workplace that you know you have offended them, stepped on toes, and in general, been difficult.

"Look for positive feedback from all sides, from people who are willing to give it in a non-threatening way," Hanson says. "But, only you know what your workplace can handle, and that's why a third party can help you facilitate the process."

And, always remember that we're all human.

"We all make mistakes. And people are going to want to believe what they've always believed about you, so it may be tough to change their minds. But if you and the group can deal with this and go on, then you're going to create a stronger bond than ever before, and then everyone benefits," Hanson says.

Still, it's not always easy admitting you've not been the nicest person to live with at work, and you might consider confiding whether other factors have played a part in your behavior—a personal problem, or perhaps a mental illness such as depression. Hanson says these issues are becoming more acceptable for discussion at work, and more people are sympathetic to such problems. If you're unsure, talk to your "third party" about it.

Hanson says that co-workers may come to understand that a lack of forgiveness and the inability to help someone who needs it—despite past behavior—can ultimately backfire.

"These days, we live in a global world, and I think everything we do has a ripple effect," Hanson says. "So it's bad for the whole group if someone has to leave because they can't make a new start. Everyone loses, because there's a sense of ownership that is lost when this person goes."

In addition, increased networking and upgraded communication skills among different workplaces can make it tough for a "difficult" personality to snag another job, since a bad reputation will be talked about among professional associates. So, it's better for your career in the long run if you deal with conflicts before moving on and continuing the cycle.

Hanson says that because he often has seen personalities clash during his 30 years of experience in the business world, he says it's important that employees are trained in conflict management, and ways to be more tolerant of others in today's fast-paced world.

Hanson points out that old assumptions in the workplace—such as thinking there is no time for socializing at work or that being emotional can prevent us from making rational decisions—must be cleared away.[2] He argues those kind of outdated ideas are what lead to unhappy employees who take out their frustrations on others, and intolerant workers who aren't willing to turn the other cheek.

Notes Hanson: "Like the gardener who removes the rocks, shrubs and debris before plowing, we must find a way to remove these false assumptions. What's more, like the gardener, we must remove them with our hands and our hearts, not just our heads. Otherwise, the roots of the problem will remain and the weeds of discontent will grow at the earliest opportunity."

Hey, Loser...Boss Wants to See You

If you've ever felt that your boss sets you up to fail, research suggests you may not be paranoid—but right.

Jean-Francois Manzoni, an assistant professor at a leading European business school, INSEAD in Fountainbleau, France, says his studies show that when an employee doesn't excel on the job, the manager does not hold himself responsible, even when it can be linked to the boss's own behavior.[3]

"They say it is the employee—the person cannot work on their own, are not responsible or are not creative," Manzoni says. "But it becomes a self-fulfilling prophecy."

What that means is that once a boss has decided a worker cannot succeed, then it becomes very difficult—if not downright impossible—to break that opinion. Specifically, the manager makes it more difficult for the employee's suggestions to see the light of day, or argues with every idea the employee makes so that it is less likely others will pick up on the idea.

"And when it becomes really bad, you become transparent," says Manzoni. "It may become so difficult that the subordinate has to leave in order to achieve anything."

The fallout is not only damaging to individual careers, but in the new work dynamic calling on team efforts, group innovations and shared information, such actions can damage other workers and ultimately, the company.

"The beauty of the research is that we found the bosses won't deny that they behaved this way. They say that they are generally aware that they behaved in more controlling ways with the lower group of performers," Manzoni says. "The bosses do what they want and they get what they expect."

As a result, even though an employee may be capable of great things, once targeted as a low performer they may begin to act that way. The person begins to doubt his or her own judgment, withdrawing and offering fewer ideas for consideration. Still others may turn the other way and begin taking on huge workloads in order to prove their worth—but quality suffers, and that only emphasizes the negative label.

In research with more than 800 business executives, Manzoni found that there is an "intervention" for bosses who are willing to admit to such destructive behavior and want to fix it. Manzoni emphasizes it must come from the top—an employee has little recourse once such action starts.

He advises an intervention should:

1. **Set a peaceful meeting site.** A time and place should be agreeable to the boss and the employee. It should be emphasized this is not a chance to give "feedback" to the employee (that often bodes ill for the worker), but rather a chance to

address the relationship in an open and honest way. The boss can admit there is tension—and that he may be responsible for problems in the employee's performance. The worker should be free to discuss the manager's behavior.

2. **Address the weaknesses.** No one sets out to fail, but sometimes employees are not as capable in some areas as in others. The boss and the worker need to decide the specific areas of weakness, and the manager needs to provide evidence that these flaws exist. This is a chance for the employee to compare his performance with others, pointing out strengths and capabilities.

3. **Find out why.** Once the performance problems have been identified, then it's time to find out why this weakness exists. Has the boss been contributing to the problem with his attitude? What assumptions by the employee and the manager have contributed to the tensions over these problems?

4. **Agree on objectives.** Once the dirty laundry has been aired, then it's time to move forward. The manager and employee should agree on performance objectives, and how their relationship can improve. While new objectives may require some monitoring by the boss, an employee should be free of intense scrutiny as the performance improves.

5. **Improve communication.** The employee and boss should agree to address any problems in the future right away, opening the door to more honest communication.

"The more I have looked at this issue systematically, the more I saw it really was a phenomenon," Manzoni says. "But it is possible to interrupt the dynamic. I'd recommend that employees who recognize it to give their bosses a copy of (our research) and see if they recognize themselves."

Excuse Me, Is That a Stapler In My Back?

Since downsizings and layoffs of the last decade eroded whatever security once existed in the workplace, it has been said that one of the most destructive fallouts has been the increased intensity of office politics.

And while the rumors and gossiping and "grapevine" communications are as common to the workplace as e-mail, unfortunately it has reached a new level of nastiness, sneakiness and viciousness. In fact, it's probably one of the greatest causes of stress for many workers who cannot concentrate fully on their jobs because they're so busy protecting their backs.

This backbiting among workers is often known as "turf wars," because people literally are protecting their turf from encroachers, although their actions usually have more far-reaching repercussions, including sabotaging other careers or hurting company profits.

"When there are limited resources and rewards in the workplace, people are going to want more, or what they feel is enough for them," says Annette Simmons, a behavioral science consultant. "People will tend to hoard and act like there are limited supplies of the things that give them power— things like information and the authority to make decisions first and relationships with others."

As a result, the organization suffers because sharing information is critical in today's fast-paced business environment, and slimy office politics direct energies away from important issues. At the same time, those on the receiving end of territorial skirmishes may find themselves shut out of key business decisions that could eventually force them to leave a company.

Such dirty tactics include monopolizing time with clients; being excessively polite when speaking with certain colleagues; inviting speculation about a new co-worker by revealing the person belongs to an Elvis fan club; or enjoying coming up with humorous put-downs concerning other employees.

Other turf battles can be characterized by scheduling meetings so someone cannot attend; or agreeing to consult with a co-worker on a proposal, then deciding at the last minute to go it alone.

Simmons says that you should be aware there are different types of players in turf wars, and your ability to recognize them may be the first step to protecting yourself. Consider these underhanded strategies she identifies:[4]

☑ **The occupation game.** Either through physical or intangible ways, someone has staked out the territory first, giving him or her ownership of something like a project or department.

☑ **The information manipulations game,** where a player denies a rival access to information about resources or opportunities, or changes a few numbers to put it in the player's favor.

☑ **"Go ahead. Make my day."** This intimidation tactic uses verbal threats and public humiliation.

☑ **The powerful alliances game.** Schmoozing the top brass is the strategy.

☑ **The invisible wall strategy.** The sneakiest game of all, it relies on the careful orchestration of policies and procedures to create as much hassle as possible for the perceived turf invader.

☑ **"Oops! I forgot!"** It may be mindless, but it works. The person agrees to cooperate, then defaults at the last minute. This also is known as lying.

☑ **Sacking the credibility.** This tarnishes the reputation of someone by questioning competence, which can then make the person angry or fearful—all pretty effective in weakening defenses.

☑ **The shunning game.** By pretending someone doesn't exist, you brand her an outsider or freeze her out through excessive politeness. A very nasty game that can break even the toughest person.

☑ **The camouflage game.** Taking a person by surprise by leading them down another path will quickly mire him/her in red tape.

☑ **Just keep talking.** The person sounds cooperative, but by talking long enough, can head anyone off. Burying someone under a barrage of words will hopefully help him/her forget his/her goals.

"The best way to deal with these games is by shifting someone from this smaller picture to the bigger picture. These kind of people are very short-sighted, so you've got to point out the bigger picture. Then hoarding turf doesn't make sense because they're cutting off their nose to spite their face," Simmons says. "You've got to expose it and deal with it, and create a sense of trust and community."

———— • ————

When Your Job Isn't Worth the Work

Next time you have a day off, forget the laundry and the garage that needs cleaning out and the work you brought home. Instead, use the time to think about what your job means to you. And don't use six seconds to say, "a paycheck" and then forget about it.

Instead, ask yourself: "Do I receive rewards from my work other than the monetary compensation?"

Your first answer may be a resounding "no" or a hesitant "yes," but chances are you've never sat down and really thought about what you do and how it makes you feel—and if you can or should change that reality.

Geoffrey M. Bellman, a workplace consultant, says that people often make the mistake of concentrating only on how much money they make when determining their job satisfaction. "You're looking at what you think you deserve, in terms of pay, and that puts the focus on the employer, not on yourself. So from the beginning, you're playing from the employer's structure. That's the beginning of making yourself a victim," he says.

And while no one dismisses the importance of bringing home enough money to support a family or pay bills, you actually may get a better picture of your on-the-job rewards if you look at the other things important to you at work: respect, fairness, training and professional growth.

"Money is an area legitimate to gripe about and talk about," Bellman says. "It's easier to say you deserve more money than it is to say you deserve more job satisfaction. Respect and fairness are kind of squishy words."

Well, squishy or not, it's those kind of things that seem to matter when we get right down to it. So get some paper and a pen, and let's look at where you are and where you want to be and how you feel about the whole workplace deal these days.

Using some assessment tools provided by Bellman,[5] consider:

1. **Has your job been rewarding lately?** For all that effort that you put into it, what do you get back? Are those rewards important to you? Think about where the rewards come from—your boss, your employees, your customers or your peers. Now think about how these rewards make you dependent or independent, and if you had only yourself to count on for rewards, would you be satisfied?

2. **If you'd like to see some of those rewards change, how would you change them?** Go ahead and write down your fantasy—there's probably some realistic expectations in there somewhere. When looking at your dream changes, how would they affect your dependence on, or independence from, others?

3. **If you went after these new, changed rewards, what kinds of action would be required of you that are different from those you are taking now?** Don't worry about the risks right now. Just concentrate on how you would get some of those positive changes in your life. Imagine yourself in those situations that might get you those rewards, and what you would be doing.

4. **Make a list of what the risks would be if you went after the reward, of acting to get the work satisfaction you are seeking.** How could it hurt you or others? Decide how big a risk it is, and what are your chances of success? Would it be worth it?

5. **What does all this thinking suggest as action?** What do you want to do? What will you do?

Keep in mind that once you feel you've answered these questions, it does not mean you rush into action. Bellman says you should use this exercise as a chance to perhaps gain a new perspective on what you do, and perhaps preparing yourself for change.

"You need to keep this list alive, and return to it regularly—sometimes even daily—to see if your work it motivating you. Think about who else you could involve to change things, or what you can do for yourself that day to improve it," Bellman says.

He cautions, however, not dwelling on the salary issue every day, since that is something that may be out of your control until pay evaluation time rolls around each year. "Often, we get caught up in thinking that money shows us in some way that we're at least valuable for that moment," he says. "We're hungry for recognition, and money may be the only way we think we get it. Pay does not represent your self-worth."

Still, some people may find after completing the job satisfaction exercise that no amount of money can fill the gaping holes of their unhappiness at work.

If that's the case, Bellman says, then it may be time to move on.

"You give over half your waking hours to work, so wouldn't it be nice if it was tied to fulfillment in your life? Now is the time to start taking concrete steps to look at that and see if there is a solution for you. Explore your options," he says.

Searching For a Job Is a Job

Job hunting can be exhilarating, rewarding and satisfying. It also can be humiliating, demoralizing and exhausting—and that's why it's important you don't lose your grip while searching for your next position.

One of the biggest mistakes job hunters make is paying attention only to the "mechanics" of searching for work, such as composing the perfect resume, practicing for the perfect interview and networking like a maniac.

So just stop it. And keep this in mind: you cannot lose control of your life just because you're looking for a new job. Because once you lose control of your life, you lose control of your search.

Carla-Krystin Andrade, a physical therapist and psychotherapist known for her seminars for job hunters, says people looking for work lose control for many reasons. For example, job hunters lose their daily routine, either through job loss or because they are overloading their schedule trying to look for other work while still employed.

Because this loss of structure makes a person more vulnerable, it's inevitable that job seekers lose confidence and lose sight of what they're looking for.

"There are critics all around you," Andrade says. "And the worst critic is yourself."

Further, job hunters often make the mistake of putting everything in life on hold while they search for work. Motivation begins to lag without the structure of goals and a daily routine. Add to that the fact that job seekers often let themselves go physically by living on junk food and not exercising, and you've got the recipe for stress.

Andrade says the key is to treat job hunting as a job. Recognize the skills required to look for work, and remember each day how much you're doing to try and find work. This is especially critical for those who have been looking for work for more than a year. And while you're at it, tell that inner critic of yours to shut up. Write down all the negative things you're saying to yourself for a week, then go over the list and remind yourself of your strengths.

Some other pointers:[6]

- ☑ **Maintain your self-respect.** Even though you lost a job, you are still a worthwhile person. Don't let rude interviewers get you down.

- ☑ **Be good to yourself.** "Reward yourself each day that you search," Andrade says.

- ☑ **Take care of your body.** Eat right and get enough exercise and rest.

- ☑ **Don't neglect your personal life.** Take the time to nourish friendships as well as business relationships. Set goals for improving the quality of your personal life.

- ☑ **Let go of the past.** This will help you focus on the positive side of a job search, making you more effective.

- ☑ **Ask for, and accept, support from the people in your life.** Remember that they care about you, not your financial condition.

☑ **Listen and learn from other people's success stories.** Use the lessons they learned to further your own success.

———◆·◆———

The More We Know, The More We Fret

Most of us can clearly remember the first job interview we ever had. Maybe it was for a position flipping hamburgers or perhaps as a clerk in a small bookstore. More than likely, you weren't too nervous because you were too young (and naïve) to consider the consequences of doing poorly in an interview.

Today, the story has changed. People who are in the middle of their lives—and careers—are going through job interviews again as they face the painful reality that no job lasts forever. And learning that a lousy interview can land you back on the street.

"The biggest mistake people make in interviewing is deciding to wing it," says Paul D. Green, an expert on interviewing. "People think they can just do their best rather than just do their best with preparation. The three keys to good interviews are to prepare, to prepare, to prepare."

Green, who has educated managers for 25 years on how to interview and hire the right person and has interviewed more than 5,000 people, says that the biggest challenge is for the job candidate to "build a rapport faster, deeper and better than the other person being interviewed."

"And you do that by being prepared to tell the interviewer what you do well," he says.

For example, even if you think you can relate all your skills well to an interviewer, you have to consider that the job market is changing so fast you may need to reposition what you know about yourself in terms of the performance skills and technical skills today's employers are looking for.

"The technological stakes are very high, and so interviewers will often question you about computer skills," Green says. "They are also going to be more structured in how they get information on performance issues such as coping, teamwork and creativity. They're going to focus on your work habits."

Green advises candidates to make a "skill-benefit statement," for the interview that 1) is a basic description of a skill you have and 2) a summary of the benefits the skill can generate, or your value to the organization. For these statements, combine "I can" with "able to." ("I can program your inventory so you will be able to reorder supplies at just the right time.")

Remember that these statements aren't a chance to brag—you're providing information to the interviewer, not waxing poetic about what a stupendous human being you are.

Green has a few other suggestions for interviews:[7]

- ☑ **Because of legal mandates, interviews will be much more focused on the job requirements and less on your personal lifestyle and values.**

- ☑ **Try to find out in advance what the job involves.** Then prepare statements that emphasize the skills you have most relevant to the position. If the organization is moving to team-based management, stress the experience you have in that area.

- ☑ **Without sounding negative, compare or contrast your work with the good work of others.** Try not to sound critical of co-workers or your organization, but compare your skills with a higher standard to show them in a better light to the interviewer.

- ☑ **Bring a work sample to the interview** and describe the skills you used in developing it.

- ☑ **Don't give the interviewer the impression you are solely responsible for your success.** Describe the opportunities you were given, then explain what you did to take advantage of them.

- ☑ Either consciously or unconsciously, **interviewers are influenced by body language.** Keep your hands away from your face, sit up, lean forward and nod affirmatively to reflect confidence and pride.

Over 50 and On the Job Road Again

Looking for a job is certainly no bed of roses for anyone, but it can be more difficult for older Americans. Perhaps they have given decades of dedicated service to one company, only to find themselves in the job market at a time when they expected to be planning a comfortable retirement.

The feelings of anger, betrayal and depression that all workers experience when they lose a job often are debilitating to those over 50. Not only do they not know where to begin, but they might face age discrimination when they do make inquiries about employment.

And yet, there are job opportunities for older workers, and many companies are finding those employees are more stable and committed to the workplace than younger workers who are often hunting for the next job.

Catherine Dorton Fyock, who specializes in the aging and changing workforce, says that our culture values youth, and that makes it tough for older employees to find new positions.

"But a lot of managers are frustrated by the work ethic of younger workers, and older workers offer them a chance to hire people with an old-fashioned work ethic," she says.

One of the biggest problems for older Americans looking for work is that they simply do not know where to begin. Job-hunting is much different than it was a decade ago, and older workers just need to refine their job search skills to meet market demand.

Fyock advises workers to take the initiative and position themselves for opportunities. If they are still employed, she says, they should take advantage of any and all training offered at the company. If they are unemployed, she says, they should use their time to assess their skills and draw on those strengths.

"Ask friends and family about your strengths," Fyock says. "Sometimes seeing yourself from another person's point of view can be helpful."

In addition, Fyock recommends older Americans looking for work can do the following:[8]

☑ **Network.** Think of all the contacts made with suppliers, customers, co-workers and community leaders over the years. Call each of them and let them know you're looking for work.

☑ **Research companies in your area.** Visit the local library so that you are well-informed about the industry, who is in charge of hiring and what the employment needs are.

☑ **Attend a career fair.**

☑ **Look everywhere.** Check out employment opportunities on the Internet, through newspapers and professional publications, newsletters and employment agencies.

☑ **Go back to school.** No one is too old to learn. Check with a university or community agency to find out what learning opportunities are available. Now is the chance to hone your computer skills.

☑ **Consider an informational interview.** Not all employers are willing to offer one, but you can request an interview where you ask the questions. Inquire about opportunities in the career you are considering, and prepare your questions carefully. Don't take more than 20 minutes of the company representative's time, and take careful notes.

☑ **Temporary, part-time and volunteer work all offer employers a chance to see what you're made of**—and that you're perfect for a full-time position.

☑ **Don't be desperate.** Nothing scares off a job offer faster. By doing your homework, you approach job openings with confidence, and that makes a good impression on an interviewer.

Notes Fyock: "Looking for a job is the most difficult job many of us will ever have. There are so many techniques being used that we have to personally take more responsibility for our own future, and our own skills update. We have to pursue every opportunity."

When the Blues Won't Go Away

We've all had those days when we sit down at our desks and shuffle papers for several minutes, unable to really concentrate and feeling a bit overwhelmed by the work staring us in the face.

But for many workers, this problem is chronic. Instead of gaining their focus after a few moments, their inability to concentrate only gets worse. Their energy level drops, they may have trouble sleeping or eating. In addition, they may have feelings of guilt, lack of self-worth or a feeling of helplessness.

These symptoms lasting over several weeks can signal a serious, but treatable medical illness known as clinical depression. And in more workplaces around the country, employers are being educated about the signs of this illness so workers may get the needed treatment.

One of the reasons for this educational effort is that many employees try to hide their problems, avoiding their managers and co-workers. Not only is their work performance adversely affected by this illness, but clinical depression contributes to nearly half of this nation's suicides.

The Wellness Councils of America (WELCOA) in Omaha, Neb., says that one in 10 Americans will experience clinical depression, which can translate into nearly $27 billion a year in worker absenteeism, lower productivity and healthcare costs. And while employee assistance programs list clinical depression as one of the top five problems reported by workers, often the problem goes unnoticed in the workplace.

WELCOA believes that educating managers about clinical depression and its warning signs can get workers into treatment sooner and save the careers and jobs of those who have this illness.

Among the warning signs of clinical depression:

- ☑ **Difficulty in making decisions.**
- ☑ **Decreased productivity.**
- ☑ **Irritability and hostility.**
- ☑ **Withdrawal from others** or, conversely, **extreme dependence on others.**

- ☑ Feelings of hopelessness or despair.

- ☑ Slowness of speech, chronic fatigue.

- ☑ Slumping posture, flat or blank facial expression.

- ☑ Inability to concentrate, decline in dependability.

- ☑ Unusual increase in errors in the work product.

- ☑ Proneness to accidents.

- ☑ Tardiness, absenteeism.

- ☑ Lack of enthusiasm for work tasks.

Experts say that despite the fact that depression is an illness that responds to treatment in up to 90 percent of cases, fewer than 40 percent of the 17 million Americans who suffer from it each year will seek treatment.

Out of Sight, Out of Mind

In today's virtual workplace, we can be 10,000 miles from the home office but still communicate effectively and efficiently with company brass using teleconferencing capabilities. We can fire off e-mails and voice mails to support staff, and with the click of a mouse, network with colleagues around the world.

Technology, for those reasons and more, is a terrific business tool. But for some companies, it is becoming a potential menace as workers become isolated, less productive and possibly even depressed by the overuse of computers, faxes, e-mails and voice messaging.

Specifically, a study by Carnegie Mellon University found that people who spend even a few hours a week on the Internet suffer higher levels of depression and loneliness. And there seem to be plenty of horror stories about careers gone awry when unwitting employees working from home simply stop showing their faces at the office, or fail to keep up on office politics and stumble into delicate situations.

Such scenarios are becoming more common since it's estimated that 11.1 million people telecommuted in 1997, triple the number in 1990. Despite those numbers, it seems that there are many workers—and companies —unprepared for the unique struggles associated with these arrangements, says Dr. Val Arnold, a management expert.

Arnold says that bosses may have difficulty giving up the control that comes with facing workers every day in the workplace, and employees often underestimate their own need for interaction and networking—the social aspects that come from working each day with other people.

"You can lose sight of the fact that what you do is part of the organizational puzzle if you don't see people often," he says. "That's why I strongly recommend that even if you work away from the office, that you periodically go into work and see people."

Arnold recommends that even the most "far-flung" workers visit their workplace at least once a quarter, and "any less than that and you've fallen off the map." He notes that those who are a great distance from their home office should negotiate how many return visits the company will pay for when they begin such an arrangement.

At the same time, Arnold says that those working from satellite locations mistakenly believe they can bond electronically with other people through e-mails, when a close connection only will be achieved through frequent phone calls and face-to-face meetings.

"When you cannot be in the office too often, aim to attend the big things, like the kick-off meeting for a big project, or a staff meeting, or something where you'll have a chance to see a lot of people," he says. "When you're out of sight, then you start getting excluded from things, like promotions or important decision-making meetings."

Still, it can be tough to stay in touch for many employees and so they may come to rely on a trusted co-worker to keep them up-to-date.

"But then you get into the issue of how you pay these people back," Arnold says. "Think of it in terms of the currencies you have to trade. For example, you can share information with them, or help them out on a project when they need it. You've got to find that support network and then do your best to help others as they help you."

Experts also recommend that companies do a better job of finding those geared for telecommuting. For example, those who have demonstrated an ability to clearly define work objectives, are organized, results-oriented and manage time well are much better suited than those who can easily lose focus and don't have a clear in-depth knowledge of their job and their company's mission.

"I think one of the biggest problems for people who work from home is not setting boundaries for themselves, such as their times of operation and the personal standards they plan to hold—such as not working in their pajamas," Arnold says. "If you're not clear with yourself, then work spills more and more into your home life, more than it did when you worked in an office."

At the same time, management needs to be educated in telecommuting and how some of their expectations of employees may need to be altered in order to make sure the arrangement works. Many of those who work from home claim that bosses often believe they spend their time watching soap operas and taking three-hour lunches, when in reality they often work harder and more diligently at a home desk.

Arnold says the key to telecommuting success is open communication between employees and management. "It's important that you find ways to check in with your boss to keep up on what is going on, so that you can get continual feedback and keep them involved in your career," he says. "Set it up from the beginning the standards and boundaries you want and it will go much smoother for everyone."

<hr />

Behave Yourself, Even After Hours

By now, most of us (hopefully) know that making sexually suggestive remarks to a co-worker, or physically touching an employee in an intimate way is a no-no. But there are still many improvements to be made before sexual harassment is eliminated in the workplace, and perhaps no area deserves closer attention than what goes on outside the office.

How can sexual harassment in the workplace take place outside of work? Easy. Think of the office Christmas party, the company picnic, business travel and virtual offices.

It is in those settings that behavior is more relaxed, alcohol may be involved, and employees and managers may begin to discuss personal issues.

Those are the ingredients that can lead to problems, says Darlene Orlov, a sexual harassment expert.

"Lawyers report that complaints of sexual harassment spike up after the Christmas parties and company picnics," Orlov says. "Without proper training, people believe the workplace ends with the office walls."

Well, it doesn't. That means that the Friday nights you join co-workers for a good time at the local pub does not mean that you abandon the common sense you use in the office regarding your behavior. In fact, this is where you should be on guard to make sure that a few beers don't loosen your inhibitions. Offensive speech or behavior with other employees—even if you consider them friends—can come back to haunt you when a sexual harassment claim is filed.

In addition, business travel often is a minefield of problems. A manager calling a subordinate to a hotel room to deliver documents isn't a good idea, no matter how innocent the request. Always meet co-workers or employees in the hotel lobby, and have dinner in the restaurant—not in someone's hotel room.

At the same time, dinner with a clients or customer should be held in well-lit, public restaurant, and avoid any physical contact beyond a business handshake. Forget any events (such as stripper clubs) that might be embarrassing to anyone.

"It doesn't matter if you're in a plane, a train, in a hotel, a trade show or out to dinner, all the same questions are raised regarding sexual harassment," Orlov says. "And when you're together for long periods of time, you run out of business things to talk about. That's when personal talk starts—and that's a dangerous zone."

Orlov says one of the biggest problems with sexual harassment is that people remain unclear about what action they should take when they encounter questionable behavior. Many managers say they would clearly put a stop to racist remarks, but often comment they would just leave the room if talk became sexual.

"The key is that managers need to understand what sexual harassment is, and then put a stop to the behavior," she says.

Orlov says there are a ways to check out whether you are guilty of sexual harassment. Ask yourself:[9]

☑ Do I kid around in a sexual way?

☑ Do I generally direct my humor to members of the opposite sex?

☑ Do I tell racy jokes no matter who is listening?

☑ Do I think members of the opposite sex are less able than I am?

☑ Do I frequently make remarks about how people look?

☑ Do I use obscene language when things go wrong?

☑ Do I use sexual language as part of my everyday conversation?

☑ Do I tend to touch people when I talk to them?

☑ Do I tend to make comments that are a put-down to one gender?

☑ Do I ignore the no's when asking someone for a date until I get a yes?

☑ Do I use sexual comments and gestures to intimidate people or gain power?

☑ Do I ignore conduct that I really think could be sexual harassment?

Winning Doesn't Include Sleeping on the Couch

In the working world, we try not to show our weaknesses, concentrating instead on displaying our strengths. We respond to others with confident tones, argue our point of view firmly and lead with authority.

Too bad we're not always right.

This may be a hard concept to grasp for some people, especially those who have risen in the ranks because they are always right. But it is true that those who become the most rigid in their attitudes—who always have to have the right answer and must always prove others wrong—are not only annoying, but well, wrong.

Robert E. Staub II, an international consultant on leadership effectiveness, says that it is ingrained in us from the time we are young that we must strive for the "right" answer, must sit "right" and look "right"—and we will somehow be shamed for being wrong.

"We begin to confuse being right with winning," he says. "And it's not the same thing at all."

He says that executives are often the most guilty of the "always right" attitude, and can be very defensive if they are challenged. But by denying there is anything left to learn, we undermine ourselves and our companies. He says failing to acknowledge that other people may have the right answer "can lose you others' respect and de-motivate people."

"The most successful teams and the most successful individuals challenge each other to come up with the best idea and the best process," Staub says. "The key is being able to say to someone, 'you were right. That is a better idea. Thank you.'"

Staub says that letting go of being right all the time takes courage. You may have to admit that you are insecure about being "wrong," but are willing to make yourself vulnerable so that you can learn and grow.

If you realize that your "right" attitude has gone too far, Staub suggests that you can improve by:[10]

- ☑ **Admitting you have a problem.** That's half the battle.
- ☑ **Defining what winning looks like to you.** Think about what you really want, considering how you feel about an issue and what personal experiences come into play.
- ☑ **Looking at how often your need to be right really interferes with what you want.** If you shut people down by interrupting them with your "right" solution, or they turn away because you have proven them "wrong," note this interaction on a 3x5 card. Write down what happened, your reaction, and the price that was paid (de-motivation, less creative answer, etc.)
- ☑ **Defining your fear or anxiety.** If you can't be right, what will be your strategy to deal with that? Tell yourself over and over that it's okay to win, but you don't have to be right.

☑ **Beginning to ask questions.** Become curious. Those who are always right don't try to find out what other people may know. This is a chance to ask questions, then keep your mouth shut. Only after someone has given you an answer do you respond with your perspective. That starts a dialogue, and that begins the learning process.

☑ **Stepping into ambiguity.** Focus on the "shades of gray." Notice how often your thinking is automatically "right versus wrong." Argue the other side of the issue first, and look to see the larger perspective.

Staub says he learned early in his married life what the difference was between being right and winning. He says that he proved to his wife—in front of a group of friends—that he was right about an issue, and she was wrong.

"I slept on the couch that night," he says. "I was right, but I didn't win."

----◆----

Don't Let the Door Hit You on Your Way Out

One day you're sitting at work and you get this funny feeling. Something doesn't seem quite right. Maybe you dismiss it as the greasy burger you had for lunch. But the next day, the feeling is back—and you haven't had lunch yet.

It's a feeling that something is wrong. Again, you may try to ignore it. But if you're smart, you'll listen to what your gut is trying to tell you—that you're about to get canned.

"Your rational mind and maybe your spouse will tell you that you're crazy, so you'll discount the feeling," says Richard M. Contino, a lawyer. "You don't want to cope with the change that will happen when your income stops and your life comes crashing down."

But with no job guaranteed these days, it's simply good career management to know when work is going so wrong that you may be forced into resigning, or be fired outright.

Contino says men often will confront a boss, being aggressive and very direct about whether they are about to lose a job. The result: denial by the manager who dislikes such directness. Women may be less direct, and fail to ask the manager directly about their job status. The result: denial by a boss who dislikes such passive behavior.

The way to get an answer, Contino says, is to calmly ask a co-worker or boss: "Do you think something is wrong?"

If it appears that there is indeed something very, very wrong, then it's time to gather your forces. That means finding quiet time to think and come up with a contingency plan, whether it means getting your resume together, contacting a headhunter to help you find another job, or interviewing with companies in the area.

Contino stresses that the reason it is so important to listen to your intuition is that such insight may buy you the time you need to search for a new job before you are terminated, or make it easier to negotiate a better deal when you leave on your own terms.

Experts say that employers often are willing to offer severance packages to employees who are willing to leave before being fired. Consider asking for:

- ☑ **Cash.** Contino says it is typical to offer a month's pay for every year of employment.

- ☑ **Healthcare coverage.** Companies may be willing to extend coverage and pick up your cost for a specific amount of time.

- ☑ **Stock options.** This may include accelerating vesting, or receiving additional vesting as part of a severance package.

- ☑ **Vacation and sick days.** If your company does not have a written policy against it, you may be able to get paid for the days you have not taken.

- ☑ **Pensions.** Ask for continued membership in a pension or retirement plan, which may mean the company continuing its contribution for you or matching any contributions you make, for as long as you receive severance pay.

- ☑ **Job-hunting advantages.** Consider what options are available to you that will enhance your search for a new job. Perhaps you can ask for continued use of the company's on-site daycare while you look for work, or receive discount office supplies you will need to prepare resumes. Maybe you would still like to attend a trade show you were scheduled for that now will offer you numerous networking opportunities for finding a new position.

Remember that when a company fires you, do not sign anything right away until you have had a chance to fully evaluate your situation. When the employer begins negotiating your severance package, take notes so that you can clearly recall later what is on the table. Finally, it's a good idea to have a lawyer look over an negotiated agreement to make sure there are no problems and you are being treated fairly.

Putting the Right Spin On a "De-Hiring"

When interviewing for a job, most people get a little nervous. And if you've recently been laid off or fired from your last position, that fear may escalate to King Kong proportions because you may be concerned the interviewer will not see you as a viable candidate if you are currently without work.

But there is a way to put a positive spin on the fact your last job was eliminated and you've been without work for nine months, or that you were fired.

Paul Green, an interviewing expert, says that if you have been fired or laid off, the important thing to bring to an interview is how you used that experience to improve yourself.

Specifically, he advises that you refer to your termination as "de-hiring,"—and simply present the logic of how it happened in four or five sentences. If you have been laid off, there will be a certain degree of understanding from the interviewer since it has been more common in the last decade.

"But never, never say you were fired," Green says. "Don't ever say that word, because it will alarm the interviewer and they won't hear anything after that."

Instead, Green advises that you say "you left by mutual agreement," and "present what happened—but don't sound defensive or cast blame."

He also says that you can tell an interviewer that you received a "tremendous" severance package that you decided to accept—if that is what happened.

He says that some interviewers may ask what you did to cause a de-hiring, and this is where your previous rehearsal of answers will become critical.

"You practice, practice, practice all your answers to questions," he says. "Then get a friend to listen to you, or record yourself on videotape. Don't put your hands on your face, because it makes you look defensive. It's important that you be honest because that helps you maintain your dignity and that's what will come across."

If an interviewer questions you about a period that you were unemployed, you can respond that you used it to pursue additional education, or that you used it as family time to reassess your life and carefully plan your future.

"If you worked on a degree during this period, you can say that you wanted to just go to school for a time and get a jumpstart on your next position," Green says. "Or, if you were just at home, it is now reasonably acceptable to say that you were taking time for your family and you were looking at options. Express it as a real act of courage, that it's difficult to take the time to look ahead, but that's what you did."

Then, describe the outcome of these situations—you've furthered your education or you've had some very meaningful time with your family that has crystallized your future plans.

Green calls this a time to "SHARE"—a process that allows you to give the interviewer comprehensive examples of times you used specific skills. Here's how it works:

- ☑ **Situation:** Begin by describing the situation in which you were operating.

- ☑ **Hindrance:** Describe any constraints or hindrances on your actions.

- ☑ **Actions:** Explain exactly what you did.

- ☑ **Results:** Describe the results that can be attributed to your actions.

- ☑ **Evaluation:** Summarize the example with a positive evaluation of your skill.

Green advises preparing 15-20 honest and complete examples of times when you used different skills at work or in your personal life. By having these clear-cut examples on the tip of your tongue, you have a better chance of answering difficult questions in an interview, and by sounding more confident.

"By ending with a positive statement, most interviewers will then tag onto that," he says. "You always want to end each answer on a good note."

NOTES

[1] Andrew J. DuBrin, *Your Own Worst Enemy* (Amacom, 1992)

[2] Daniel S. Hanson, *Cultivating Common Ground* (Butterworth-Heinemann, 1997)

[3] Jean-Francois Manzoni and Jean-Louis Barsoux, *Harvard Business Review* Reprint 98209

[4] Annette Simmons, *Territorial Games* (Amacom, 1998)

[5] Geoffrey M. Bellman, *Getting Things Done When You Are Not in Charge* (Berrett-Koehler, 1992)

[6] Carla-Krystin Andrade, *Stay in Control* (DBM, 1994)

[7] Paul Green, *Get Hired!* (Bard, 1996)

[8] Catherine Dorton Fyock and Anne Marrs Dorton, *UnRetirement* (Amacom, 1994)

[9] Darlene Orlov and Michael T. Roumell, *What Every Manager Needs to Know About Sexual Harassment* (Amacom, 1999)

[10] Robert E. Staub II, *The 7 Acts of Courage* (Executive Excellence, 1999)

5

COMMUNICATION

As a journalist, I spend a lot of time communicating. I've visited farmers and felons, custodians and congressmen, police officers and presidents. I spend hours on the telephone interviewing people, I answer and send queries via e-mail and keep my fax humming. So you'd think with all that practice, I'd be good at getting my message across.

But like everyone else, I can get my wires crossed in a busy day. I might have someone return a phone call and have no memory of who he or she is, or why I called in the first place. I can get confused about various time zones and call someone at 6 a.m. and not 10 a.m. as planned. (Security guards who answer the phone always like to say, "Do you know what time it is?")

Communications can be as frustrating for me as for anyone else. I've been known to respond to confusing e-mail messages with a pointed "Huh?" And don't get me started on voice-mail. There are many companies out there today who have no intention of letting you speak to a human being, and keep you on some meaningless message treadmill that has you throwing the phone receiver across your desk.

I've sat in endless meetings where I've become so frustrated with the pointless, endless gabbing that I want to take a rolled up newspaper and smack a few people across the nose. I've been in government hearings that are the national cure for insomnia.

And while I think that technology has created some wonderful opportunities for improving communications—especially for far-flung businesses—I want to scream at those who cannot remove their fannies from a chair and walk across the hall to give a clear and simple message to someone instead of e-mailing half the office.

So. You can see I have definite pet peeves about communications. I'm not sure that I'm any better at it than anyone else, but I do try. And I think that is perhaps what is lacking most these days.

Instead of striving to truly communicate with someone else, we spend time composing memos to cover our behinds; draft speeches that will fill the allotted time instead of working on truly engaging the audience; and use voice mail to rattle off messages and phone numbers faster than a speeding bullet.

Of course, communications is a two-way street, and I've been guilty of not making the effort to truly listen to what someone else is saying. For example, while visiting Quebec, Canada, I stopped outside a restaurant to read the menu posted in the window. After hearing French spoken first in various establishments, I quickly learned to say, "English, please," so that the speaker would know my native tongue. A nice girl standing on the front steps smiled and invited us inside.

"English, please," I said to the girl.

Her smile faltered. She looked kind of bewildered.

My husband gave me a hard nudge in the ribs. "She *is* speaking English," he hissed in my ear.

"Oh! Well, could you do it with a Southern accent?" I said, trying to cover my embarrassment.

I'm sure she thought I was some dumb American (if the shoe fits...), but it just goes to show that I wasn't really listening to her. I knew she would speak to me about the food available and try and entice me inside, just like all the other employees standing in front of all the other eating places. But I took her message for granted, figured I knew it all and had formulated my response after hearing—but not listening to her.

One of the greatest lessons you learn as a reporter is that pride has no place in communications. If you don't get what other people are saying, you ask them to repeat it until you do. Too bad if they think you're dumb, because if you try and write a story without full knowledge of your subject, you're either going to get it wrong, or your editor is going to make you feel even more stupid when she begins asking questions you cannot answer.

I've always believed that if people communicated more simply, we wouldn't have so many problems. I try to write my stories as if I was sitting across the kitchen table from my readers. I don't look for fancy words to fill the space, I don't make my sentences lengthy. My job is to take the information and communicate it in a clear, concise, accurate way.

Included in this chapter are ways to improve your communications efforts, and ways to dump some of those bad habits that are driving me—and lots of other people—nuts.

Enough said.

When in Doubt About Torture Method, Have a Meeting

Meetings at work seem to have a strange effect on people. Some sit and silently fume—watching the clock tick away as they think about the pile of work on their desk. Others fear they may at any moment leap from their chair and scream "Shut up!" at the unsuspecting speaker.

Still, there are companies that manage to run tight, efficient meetings. This may be accomplished in a variety of ways, from demanding everyone stand to muzzling anyone that has not gotten on the agenda beforehand.

"I think meetings are one of the main things people always complain about," says Donna N. Douglass, a time management expert. "A group of people meet 10 years ago about a certain thing, and before you know it, it has become a part of the routine and is still going on today."

This inability to control "meeting-itis" may reflect deeper problems than an inability to be succinct—it may show disorganization and a lack of goals.

"People get caught up in the busyness of the day, and something that could be handled with a phone call or by two people getting together, ends up adding more people—which means more relationships—and that means it becomes more complicated," Douglass says.

Instead, Douglass says, no one should attend a meeting without being able to contribute something specific, and any gathering that turns into a free-for-all is a clear indication that there are more people meeting in one room than is necessary.

The number of meetings can be daunting. It's estimated that managers can spend up to 50 percent or more of their week in meetings, while executives can spend up to three-fourths of their weeks in meetings. All agree on one thing: most of those sessions are a waste of time.

Douglass, with her husband Merrill, has spent many years tracking what gripes people most about meetings. See if any of these sound familiar: meetings with no purpose or no agenda; meetings that don't stick to the agenda or start late; meetings that are too long; key people missing; redundant, rambling discussions; hidden agendas; and a domination of the meeting by a few people.

If that sounds like meetings you attend or conduct, don't give up. There is hope for productive, time-efficient gatherings. Try these tips by Douglass:[1]

☑ **Set an agenda.** Invite participants to contribute items and distribute them early so everyone has time to prepare. This agenda should clearly indicate the purpose of each topic and the direction of the discussion. Also, include the results, actions or decisions expected and how much time for each item will be allotted.

☑ **Set a time limit.** Most meetings could achieve their purpose in less time. In setting time, be realistic.

☑ **Start on time.** Consider fining those who are late and using the money for charity, office parties, etc. Or, consider rewarding those who are early. Some companies have locked the door to latecomers or forced the laggards to stand during the entire meeting.

☑ **Get everyone's input.** There are wallflowers, know-it-alls and quarrelers in every group. The trick is to find the strength of each person's contribution, then effectively interrupt when the discussion heads in the wrong direction. Participants should be encouraged to talk about their feelings and opinions, not just the facts.

☑ **Make it productive.** If there's a point that is unclear, it should be clarified by providing an analogy or some other way to explain it.

☑ **Take breaks.** After 45 minutes, let participants get up and stretch their legs.

I Have No Idea What You Just Said

Information can move at high speed these days. We send memos zooming over electronic mail, we whip important documents through a fax and we tap into the Internet in seconds. And yet, our mouths are not capable of all that zooming and whipping and tapping. We still have to speak at a rate that people can understand, and make sure that what we say gets us what we want.

Easier said than done.

Judith C. Tingley, a psychologist and corporate consultant, says that the fast-paced business world has made it more difficult for us to talk to one another. To be heard today, Tingley says, workers must learn to communicate more rapidly, clearly and directly.

"There are a lot of things going on in the workplace that make people afraid to speak up—from the fear of being politically incorrect to the diversity issues that make it difficult to communicate with someone who may not have the same value system," she says.

If you'd like to improve your communication efforts, there are a few simple places to start. Tingley suggests:[2]

- ☑ **Say no and mean it.** Learn to say "no" first when a request is made. Then state one reason for your answer. As you get more skilled and more confident, you can refine the message a bit, but for now—say no. And don't be afraid to say no before a request comes out of someone's mouth—it only helps you stick to your plan instead of theirs.

- ☑ **Give it to 'em straight.** Give direct, positive and negative feedback, even if it's not in your job description. Remember that most people appreciate hearing the truth. Begin such statements with "I" and deliver your message in a way that isn't mean-spirited in its honesty.

- ☑ **Learn to survive the indirect hit.** Everyone has come up against a person who takes them off-balance with a mixed message that often leaves them feeling criticized and confused. Once you're wise to the tactic, try responding with a statement to the question asked, beginning with "I."

  For example, an indirect hit may be: "How did you enjoy your two-hour lunch?" Your response should be something like: "I appreciate your candor, but I think I'm the best judge of how I use my time." Act as if the message were straightforward instead of mixed. Or, answer the question literally and ignore the other subtle message, which may or may not be intended as criticism.

"Yes," you say. "I enjoyed my lunch."

If this fails, you can always go the "broken record" route. State your belief that there seems to be a problem, and keep that refrain going until the indirect assault seems to stop.

For example: "I feel uncomfortable when you ask me about my two-hour lunch. I'd like you to let me know directly if my going out for a long lunch is a problem from your point of view."

☑ **When the boss is gunning for you, stay calm.** When under verbal assault, don't offer justifications, apologies or qualifiers, because there is no way to win with a person who yells opinions. (In your mind, keep telling yourself what a jerk this person is.) One technique is to admit there might be some truth to what the attacker is saying—it buys you time and can turn down the intensity. Look at the bright side—at least everything is out in the open and not secret or uncertain.

Tingley also offers a few gems for helping you stay calm: "For someone to be that irritable, he must be awfully unhappy." Or, "This could be a testy situation, but I believe in myself," "This is going to upset me, but I know how to deal with it," and "If I start to get angry, I'll just be banging my head against the wall."

Notes Tingley: "We need to remember that the No. 1 problem in the workplace today is communication. People need to understand and talk to one another—it's critical to their success."

———————◆———————

It's What You Don't Say That May Get You Into Trouble

You are confused when you believe you aced a job interview, then didn't get the job. Or, you spent weeks researching a topic so you could respond intelligently in a meeting, then the boss never even solicits an opinion from you.

What's going on here? Well, it might be that your nonverbal skills need some work.

Nadine M. Grant, a communications expert, says that what you're not saying can cause big problems. The failure to communicate non-verbally, she says, is "the silent shout."

"Research shows that 58 percent of our message is based on the non-verbal—people basing an opinion of us based solely on what they see," Grant says.

She says there are three types of nonverbal action that need to be addressed to improve communications:

1. **Appearance.** Although many workplaces have eased dress restrictions, Grant says that can often backfire on women. She says that because men still wield a lot of power on the job they often can get by with a more casual attitude toward dress. But women—who may adamantly argue they should be able to dress as they wish—can be perceived as sloppy or irresponsible or disrespectful if they try to "dress down" too much.

    "I know that some women get really hostile talking about dress," Grant says. "But the truth is—even though it may seem unfair—there is a credibility factor. We want our appearance to show respect for others and send the right message."

    Employees can strike the right balance by studying the dress habits of those they want to emulate. If a boss wears more conservative clothing, think along those lines. And if you're still unsure, always go with a classic style that would be appropriate year after year.

    "Remember that someone may feel uncomfortable with you and not even know why—but it's the way you're dressed," Grant says. "Dress appropriately for a situation. For example, if you're a doctor, don't see patients while wearing golf or tennis clothes. Put on a white coat and look professional—like the patient means more to you than your game."

2. **Body language.** "We have to be really careful what we read into body language," Grant warns. "If we interpret one message only, it may be the wrong one."

For example, we may think a person who listens with arms folded is telling us they are bored. But this person may simply be cold or tired. In addition, men and women use body language differently.

"In my opinion, trying to read body language is an inaccurate science, and you must be aware of the gender differences before you jump to conclusions," Grant says.

3. **Conduct and manners.** This is often a touchy subject. Men can be afraid of opening a door for a woman at work or provide any kind of assistance because they fear being branded sexist. A simple rule: If you are helping someone because they need it—male or female—you can't go wrong.

Grant likes to refer to her "platinum rule,"—"treat people the way they want to be treated and not the way you want to be treated."

Further, don't monopolize someone's time, listen politely, take care of a dinner check if needed and use good manners.

"I think conduct and manners are definitely worse than they used to be," Grant says. "Companies want these to be givens with employees, but they're not. These are learned skills, and successful people learn them."

As for those who say that nonverbal communications like etiquette and manners aren't that important to business, Grant has this reminder: "Etiquette is a way of showing courtesy and respect for people. They're not just made up to make people feel uncomfortable. You must observe people's differences and needs and then respond in a way they want to be treated."

News Flash: Men And Women Have Trouble Understanding Each Other

All is not well between men and women in the workplace.

This probably is not big news to most people, unless you spend most of your time counting paperclips and hiding in your cubicle. But those in the trenches know it can sometimes be open warfare between the sexes. And one of the big reasons for that is that men and women have trouble communicating.

"If the East and West Germans can learn to get along, and so can the Arabs and the Jews; I don't see why men and women can't," says Judith Tingley, a psychologist. "It's causing a tremendous amount of stress in the workplace for women—but less so for men."

Men, Tingley explains, aren't as stressed because they're too paralyzed by the fear of saying or doing something that will get them branded as sexist pigs.

Tingley says that these communication problems can be eased through "genderflexing," which she says is the ability to "temporarily communicate using behaviors typical of the opposite gender in order to increase the potential for influence."

In other words, women need to be able to talk about money, business and sports, while directly stating their opinions. Men need to learn to talk about feelings, families and relationships, while being less competitive, offering feedback and asking questions.

"There are some mistaken cases of sexual harassment because men just don't get it," Tingley says. "Men will see a woman being friendly and perceive it as sexual interest. Women simply see it as being friendly. At the same time, women need to be tough with men who are coming on to them by telling them to just cut it out, and that they don't like it."

Tingley does see the sexes being able to get along, partly because both men and women are seeing these workplace wars as "ridiculous." Also, as more women become bosses, men need to learn to communicate better with them as a matter of survival.

Still, she admits it won't be easy. Tingley says some men are angry at women because they see females as interlopers getting good jobs only because they're women. On the other hand, some women are angry at men because they think males should be gentlemen and accept the successes of women.

"Women think men should recognize that a female got the job because she's better at it," Tingley says. "Men think they're victims of reverse discrimination."

To avoid communication problems in the workplace between the sexes, Tingley suggests men:[3]

1. **Think about women as business beings rather than sexual beings.**

2. **Recognize that women are as unique among their gender group as are men.**

3. **Communicate to women based on their individuality,** rather than as members of a stereotypical group.

4. **Use general humor, not aggressive sexual humor.** Be self-deprecating.

5. **Even when intentions are good, the impact of your communication may be bad.**

6. **When in doubt, don't say or do what you were thinking of saying or doing.** If not in doubt, get in doubt.

For women, Tingley suggest they improve communications with men by:

1. **Trying to remain bland when you want to express your feelings.** Men can see women as overemotional when "feelings" come into play.

2. **Expressing feelings verbally rather than nonverbally.** Men aren't good (although they're getting better) at reading behavior.

3. **Cutting back on male-bashing.**

4. **Adding humor, but not self-effacing humor.**

5. **Saying what needs to be said concisely,** without excessive apologies or disclaimers.

6. **Recognizing that many men often don't understand the impact of their sexually related comments.** If you are offended, say something directly at the time of the comment or behavior.

Help! I'm Under the Paperwork and I Can't Get Up!

If you feel like the gray matter in your head is about to explode, then you're probably suffering from a common ailment these days: information overload.

It seems like every minute of a day is now filled with e-mails and faxes and phone calls and data downloaded from the Internet and the latest statistics and company reports and...whew! More paperwork and input than we could ever hope of knowing.

In fact, many of us are "overwhelmed, buried and discouraged" by too much information, says Lynn Lively, a national speaker and writer.

How do you know if you suffer from such a condition? Consider these symptoms:

☑ You miss a deadline and claim it's because you were never told. Then you discover the date written on the second page of the assignment report.

☑ Returning from a conference, you're filled with enthusiasm and great ideas. A week later, the great ideas are sitting on a shelf because you've been swamped trying to clear off the information that piled up on your desk while you were gone.

☑ You lie awake at night wondering where a confidential file has been misplaced.

☑ The boss asks for a report and you can't put your hands on it.

☑ A promotion is lost because someone else was caught up on work and eagerly expressed a desire for a new assignment.

☑ You need a technician to help with your computer work.

☑ You fear your value to the organization is slipping because you don't have time to stay ahead of the curve when it comes to your field of expertise.

"People keep beating themselves up because they feel they can't keep up," Lively says. "You can't know it all—but you can know what you need."

Lively says the first thing you must do is eat. Or, rather, take yourself to lunch so you can have a quiet hour to reflect on what you need to know.

"You need to look at the three key aspects of your job," Lively says. "Look at those things that are essential for your success, the areas where you need to improve and your future development—what you need to keep growing."

Once you have accomplished that, then get out your crystal ball and look at the next year, and possibly into the next five years.

"Ask yourself what information knowledge you need in the future to make yourself competitive," Lively says. "This may include learning how to use the Internet, or becoming more familiar with certain software."

Once lunch is finished, you're ready to go back to work and tackle the piles of information "with tremendous focus and clarity," she says.

"Make a visual sweep of your office and imagine what it looks like without the paper. Focus on the way the office is set up—where the stuff is and how the work is done. Group the information where it makes sense—put information that is similar together."

For example, if you keep all videotapes in one place, all computer discs in another and all periodicals in another space, it may make more sense to group those items according to subject, such as teamwork.

Lively recommends people view information for what it is—knowledge expressed in any form. It is not a big, bad creature seeking to destroy us.

"Information is value-neutral. It's just out there. We may get frustrated at our ability to manipulate it, but information is not the problem," Lively says.

So the next time you feel yourself being sucked into the information vortex, remind yourself of Lively's criteria for "good" information. It must be 1) current; 2) sufficient; 3) essential;) reliable and 5) verifiable.

If it's not, you can live without it.

Stephen King Should Write About Voice Mail

See if this sounds familiar:

"Hello. This is Kathy Smith. I'm not available. Please call John White at extension 532."

"Hello. This is John White. I'm not available. Please call Kathy Smith at 235."

Or, how about:

"This is XYZ Corporation. Of the following 15 options, please choose one. When you have entered your selection, enter your PIN number, your name, followed by the pound key and your mother's maiden name followed by the star key."

Welcome to voice-mail hell.

"One time it actually took me eight months at one company to get a live person on the phone," says Dianna Booher, a communications expert. "I put in 12 calls over five months and the last call finally routed me back to the first person I talked to."

No one can dispute the fact that voice mail can be a wonderful thing—when it isn't running amok. Same thing with e-mail. What a great way to communicate with others inside and outside your company! Until you come in one morning to find 236 messages clogging your computer.

Booher says that voice-mail and e-mail are driving people batty, and horror stories abound.

"Voice-mail and e-mail are here to stay, but they need to get better," she says. "I've heard of people being on hold for 45 minutes and e-mail messages that are rambling and confusing."

She says there are easy ways to make improvements to modern communications. For example, voice-mail can be more effective if:

☑ **The message is current.** Each day, record a message stating the date and day, where you are (traveling, in a meeting) and when you will be checking for messages. Keep it short, and do not record your personal philosophy of life. Don't even think about sneaking in a sales pitch.

☑ **The customer's terminology is used,** not the company's.

☑ **Those leaving a message state it slowly and clearly,** taking time to repeat a phone number or spell a name.

☑ **It is never used to dodge calls.** Pick up your messages as soon as possible.

And for e-mail, Booher offers this advice:

☑ **Put the urgency of your message in the subject line.** Just labeling it "Atlanta conference," is not as effective as stating that "conference fees are due tomorrow."

"Many people are getting so many messages that they just look at the subject line and then delete it or print it out. The danger is that many people are not even reading messages—and there's no way of knowing what they're missing," she says.

☑ **Don't be sloppy.** E-mail, just like any other form of communication in an office, is critical. "People think because it's informal, it doesn't matter what they say," Booher says. "But if it's rambling and disorganized, then you're making a bad impression. You should consider e-mail as a valuable internal image builder."

Use proper grammar, correct spelling and capitalization. The message should be easy to read, not a minefield of errors.

☑ **Don't be cute.** It's one thing to crack a joke, tease a co-worker or use sarcasm in person. In black-and-white, however, such messages can come off as crass, unfeeling and cynical. "What you might say with a twinkle in your eye or a smile on your lips does not come across on a computer screen," Booher says.

Finally, for both voice-mail and e-mail, state whether any response is necessary so that you don't begin an endless stream of "okay, got it," messages.

Don't Read This On A Full Stomach

"Purification of unliquidated obligations is essential for the early identification and correction of invalid obligation amounts to ensure full and effective fund utilization."
—A midlevel professional at a federal agency.

Is this the kind of writing you must wade through every day? Even worse, is this the kind of noxious drivel you pride yourself on writing and sending to unsuspecting colleagues?

According to business writing experts, it's likely that you not only have to try to make sense of this kind of gobbledygook on a daily basis, but that you're probably penning some pretty putrid messages yourself.

"The biggest complaint I get is that people have to work too hard to understand what someone else is writing," says Richard Lauchman, a business writing consultant who uncovered the above passage.[4]

Joseph Dobrian, another writing consultant, agrees. "People are too verbose. They use too much business jargon, they use too many clichés and in the end, the author comes across as not very bright."

And with the increasing use of e-mail to send business correspondence, the problem appears to be growing at an alarming rate. "We typically go hog wild with e-mail, and we're much more chatty. And by the time the respondent gets through all the stuff that comes at the beginning of each e-mail, then tries to read the message, the point of it all has become nonexistent," Lauchman says.

But both experts say that whether the message is sent electronically or otherwise, business correspondence need not be painful to write (or receive) if a few simple rules are followed. Among them:

- ☑ **Use correct grammar and spelling.** If you don't know, look it up. If you're still unsure, have a trusted co-worker check it out. "You sound like an idiot when you use atrocious grammar and misspell words," Dobrian says.

- ☑ **No swearing.** "It makes many people uncomfortable and they can be offended. It's business, not a barroom," Dobrian says.

- ☑ **When smaller words will do, use them.** For example, Lauchman says writing "subsequent to," may be understood to mean "after," but if one in 100 readers misses its meaning, don't use it. (He notes that five out of 10 adult Americans either don't know what "subsequent to" means or confuse it with "before.") If a bigger word is more precise, feel free to use it.

☑ **Your entire message should be kept bare bones, in one sentence.** If you're uneasy about how to do this, imagine you have only 30 seconds to tell someone your message. That will help you zero in on the most important part.

☑ **Read your writing out loud.** The best writing often sounds as if you are speaking personally to the person. If you're gasping for breath after reading one sentence, shorten it. If it sounds awkward to say a phrase, then it's awkward to read it.

☑ **Use similes and metaphors to pep up your writing, but be conservative.** Dobrian calls these expressions the "salt and pepper of writing, not the meat!"[5]

☑ **To avoid sounding arrogant, avoid using the passive voice.** At the same time, avoid using phrases such as "for your information," "please be advised," or "obviously." These can give the reader the impression of intimidation or anger.

☑ **Break the mold.** Just because others in your company have gotten into the bad habit of using business jargon, big words and complicated sentences, does not mean you must follow their example. "It's much easier to write poorly than to write well," Lauchman says. "Don't take the easy route."

☑ **Use contractions such as "you're," "he'd," and "isn't."** It sounds much more personal and makes the writing flow more smoothly.

☑ **Remember that everything these days must be documented, and a written document lives on forever.** That makes it important not only for the future of your company, but for your career as well.

Hey Bub, The Whole World Reads Your E-Mail

We've all done it: used e-mail to send an off-color joke to a co-worker or complain about the boss or gossip about company management strategies.

This may seem relatively harmless—no one can ever find out, can they? Yes, indeed, they can.

And it can cause big, big trouble.

Just take a look at the number of recent lawsuits in the country, and you'll begin to realize that what you send as e-mail has the potential to come back and haunt you. Attorneys are using e-mail messages to prove everything from sexual harassment to pornography distribution.

It's estimated that more than one million messages pass through the Internet every hour, and an estimated 2.7 trillion e-mail messages were sent in 1997. Even more staggering: nearly 7 trillion messages are expected in the next year.

And with that increased use has come the increased risk.

"Up until about a year ago, most businesses were in a honeymoon phase with e-mail," says Michael Overly, an attorney specializing in e-mail law. "Everyone was very excited until there started being a number of lawsuits, and attorneys started focusing on e-mail. There was even a case where one attorney was sued for malpractice because he didn't investigate e-mail for his client."

Overly, special counsel to the Information Technology Department at the law firm of Foley & Lardner in Los Angeles, often advises clients on software licensing, copyright, electronic commerce and Internet and multimedia law.

He says a big problem is that many people treat e-mail "like a telephone conversation."

"I'm not saying e-mail should be abandoned, but companies need to think about informing employees about what can and cannot be sent through e-mail," he says. "We need to have some 'e-mail 101' training sessions going on."

For example, employees should be aware that even if you "kill" your e-mail, there is software available that can revive these messages even months after they were thought to be dead.

"There are firms that do nothing but specialize in retrieving electronic mail that was killed on hard disc one or two months ago," he says.

He notes that even programs designed to "shred" e-mail are not proving to be entirely foolproof. The best way to avoid problems with e-mail at work, Overly says, is to get a policy in place and make sure employees fully understand it.

Overly says employees should be educated on:

- ☑ **Informal use.** Employees often use e-mail to express thoughts, emotions and opinions that they would never put in print. But they feel free to tap a few keys and send it into cyberspace. They need to know that even if a message cannot be undeleted, backup copies of the missive may exist on the sender's or recipient's personal computer or the employer's network.

  In addition, e-mail is sent across the Internet using a protocol that has virtually no security or privacy features. So unless e-mail is specially protected, it can, and will, be read by others.

- ☑ **Lawsuit heaven.** Human resource procedures may have been followed to the letter in dismissing an employee or making sure no age discrimination laws were violated. But all it takes is e-mail containing incriminating evidence and you're in big trouble, because an attorney will go looking for it—and probably find it.

- ☑ **Freezing the system.** Just one employee using the company's system for illegal activity can result in the company's entire computer system being seized by the government to preserve evidence.

At the same time, misusing e-mail can result in litigation from other states or even other countries. Several courts have found that just sending the electronic message into their area gives them jurisdiction.

Overly says all companies (it's estimated 70 percent to 80 percent of businesses in the U.S. have access to e-mail) should immediately take steps to protect themselves from costly legal mistakes, and dangerous oversights that compromise their business, such as disgruntled employees releasing information to a competitor.

"If an employer has a policy in place, they can defend themselves in court, and also protect themselves from confidential information being disclosed," Overly says. "Most of these areas can be addressed fairly quickly and easily and if you avoided even one lawsuit, the time has been worth it."

Overly says some sample clauses in e-mail policy can include:[6]

1. **Forwarding e-mail.** Users may not forward e-mail to any other person or entity without the express permission of the sender.

2. **Chain e-mail.** Users may not initiate or forward chain e-mail. (Chain e-mail is a message sent to many people, asking each person to send copies onto another bunch of people.)

3. **Communicating information.** The content of all communications should be accurate. Users should use the same care in drafting e-mail and other electronic documents as they would for any other written communication. Anything created on the computer may, and likely will, be reviewed by others.

4. **E-mail retention.** Unless directed to the contrary by your supervisor, employees should discard inactive e-mail after 60 days.

"One of my clients has a saying that e-mail is the gift that keeps on giving—in litigation," he says. "And that's very true. Don't write anything in e-mail that you're not prepared to see in litigation."

———•———

Downloading A Virus Isn't The Only Bad News

If you have set up a World Wide Web site for your business, congratulations. You now have entered the world of cyberspace commerce, and the benefits could be terrific. But before you go willy-nilly into this exciting new world, it's important to consider the legal pitfalls of doing business through the Internet.

Legal pitfalls? What could cause problems just setting up a Web site? Plenty, says Sam Byassee, a lawyer specializing in cyberspace law.

"The number of court cases regarding the Internet is growing, and people need to be aware of some of the ways they can get into trouble," Byassee says.

Among the potentially sticky areas:

☑ **Copyright violations.** Nothing is easier than zipping through the loads of information on the Web and finding just that key bit of data you need for your Web site. But be aware that copyright laws apply to the Web, just as they do for other printed material such as magazines and books.

That means you cannot download information onto your Web site that is copyrighted by someone else, and others cannot download your copyrighted information.

"As a warning I must tell you that even though corporations are going to be liable for violating copyrights, the individual employee who actually downloaded that copyrighted information also can be held liable," he says. "Often, the individual will be sued simply as leverage to get their testimony in a copyright infringement case."

The biggest offenders: people who copy music onto their Web sites from CD-ROMs. That's a no-no, just like making copies from discs or tapes.

☑ **Owning the site.** So, you hire someone to help you design a great Web site, full of neat graphics and text, and to help you with the linkages and coding. But did you make sure that you specifically own the code and other materials that were developed? If not, then you are only licensing the materials from the developer.

"Companies will hire someone to help them, and think they have all the rights, but both sides need to really understand who owns what," he says.

☑ **Domain.** Because each Web site has a unique name, there already have been some nasty battles in court as opposing parties slug it out regarding who gets to use a specific name. For example, a company naturally wants to use its trademark name on a site, but if someone else has already claimed that domain name, then it can cause legal problems.

If you want to file for domain of a name, you must do it with InterNic (http://rs.internic.net), which currently has an agreement with the federal government to provide such a service.

However, Byassee says that people who have tried to nab a domain name with the express purpose of "selling it back" to a company will find that courts will rule against such practices.

"These people are called 'domain name pirates' and they're just hijacking names with the purpose of ransoming them back," Byassee says. "That's in violation of trademark law."

☑ **Product liability.** There are lots of things to buy on the Web, but you better make sure that whatever your company is selling does not open you up to a world of litigation. If someone in another state uses your product, and gets injured, will you be sued by that person under another state's laws? What will that cost you in terms of mounting an out-of-state defense? It's worth contemplating, especially considering the vast reach of the Internet to people all over the world.

☑ **Comments.** Many companies like having users post their opinions or ideas on Web sites, but it can lead to problems if defamatory, obscene or copyrighted material from another site is posted.

Byassee says that this is one area already generating action in the courts, and is causing friction between users and site owners. However, be aware that if you do decide to screen materials posted on your site, you will be held to a "higher standard" and may actually increase your liability risk.

☑ **Trademarks.** It isn't called the World Wide Web for nothing. You may be the only "Acme Widget Co." in the U.S., but there may be one in another part of the world that may not take kindly to you using the name—so they sue you for trademark infringement.

"I don't think that it's worth anyone's while to go after a local company that may get into some of these areas on a local basis," Byassee says. "But when you go on the Internet, your audience is much larger, and there are people who will want to enforce the federal laws. It's important to be aware of this when you have a Web site."

What Do You Mean You
Didn't Unload The Dishwasher?

You've just put in a full day on the job, and now the real work begins. You're home to face the pile of dirty dishes in the sink, the laundry that needs to be folded, a hungry family and a toilet that is making ominous sounds.

And don't forget later that your loving partner in all this is going to feel, well...loving.

Working couples today face incredible stresses as they try to juggle the demands of bosses, co-workers and the lack of time and money needed to run a household.

The unfortunate result is that marriages are breaking up, children often are neglected and a lot of people are just plain unhappy. But there are ways working couples can cope better with the demands of modern life, by learning to openly discuss how work around the house will get done in a fair way.

Jaine and James Carter, who both hold doctorates and are successful management consultants, know the demands of trying to make it all work. As parents, they concede their own children often were pushed aside as they focused on careers.

The Carters are the first to admit they did many things wrong, but they also believe they did many things right. With that in mind, they offer some advice about taking a realistic approach to marriage and careers, based on their experiences and those of hundreds of other couples who have shared their stories with the Carters.[7]

For example:

☑ **Stop being your own worst enemy.** Jaine says that women often make themselves out to be "martyrs."

"We complain that our husbands didn't do something, then we go ahead and do it ourselves," she says. "And it's all the exhausting little details that get us down."

☑ **Adjust the equation.** Jim says that men, especially younger and middle-aged males, are just learning to what it means to share home and workplace responsibilities.

"While women say they are still learning the game in the workplace, men feel the same about home responsibilities," he says. "Women need to be patient with men. Decide who will do what and then set an acceptable level of standard for, say, mopping the floor. And then just let him do it. So what if he's a little grumpy? Just let him alone and he'll get it done."

☑ **Take a meeting.** Just like at work, meet with your spouse at home to hash out the details of a project. (Unlike work, however, you can use a nice glass of wine to help relax the atmosphere.) Get a pad and pencil and decide who is going to do what.

This negotiating session should end with a commitment from each person for full responsibility of the chosen tasks and a willingness to be held accountable for lapses. Jaine suggests money in a kitty for failure to comply.

"A woman not only has to get out of her own way, but she has to stop feeling guilty about what she contributes. She also needs to remember that she is not the police officer of this relationship. If he says he's going to get something done, then he should do it," Jaine says.

The Carters believe the biggest problem for working couples today is the lack of time and money. Of the 27 million married couples who are working, the majority do so because they need the money. But because both are working, time becomes a precious commodity.

But men are learning the new routines, and it appears there may be another compelling reason they will want to comply. Notes Jaine: "Women are so angry. Because he didn't unload the dishwasher, she doesn't want to have sex with him later. They won't say that, of course. They'll say it's because they're too tired. But underneath, they're mad."

NOTES

[1] Merrill E. Douglass and Donna N. Douglass, *Time Management for Teams* (Amacom, 1992)

[2] Judith C. Tingley, *Say What You Mean, Get What You Want* (Amacom, 1996)

[3] Judith C. Tingley, *Genderflex* (Amacom, 1993)

[4] Richard Lauchman, *Plain Style* (Amacom, 1993)

[5] Joseph Dobrian, *Business Writing Skills* (Amacom, 1998)

[6] Michael Overly, *E-Policy* (Amacom, 1999)

[7] Jaine Carter and James D. Carter, *He Works, She Works* (Amacom, 1995)

About the Author

Anita Bruzzese writes "On the Job," the nation's most widely distributed workplace column. Syndicated through Gannett News Service since 1992, the weekly column has drawn interest and praise from across the country and internationally.

Besides drawing on her own expertise, Bruzzese uses her nearly 20 years of journalism experience to track down and interview those on the cutting edge of workplace issues. She is known for presenting complex issues through a down-to-earth and professional writing style.

Bruzzese writes regularly for *Human Resource Executive* and *Public HR*. Her articles have appeared in *Incentive Magazine, HR Today, The Miami Herald* and *USA Weekend*. She was the founding managing editor of *Employee Benefit News*. Prior to that, Bruzzese covered economics from the Washington bureau of Fairchild Publications, reported and edited for *USA Today* and wrote for local and daily newspapers.

Bruzzese is married to a journalist, has two sons and now lives in the Midwest.

Career Resources

Contact Impact Publications for a free annotated listing of career resources or visit the World Wide Web for a complete listing of career resources: www.impactpublications.com. The following career resources are available directly from Impact Publications. Complete the following form or list the titles, include postage (see formula at the end), enclose payment, and send your order to:

IMPACT PUBLICATIONS
9104-N Manassas Drive
Manassas Park, VA 20111-5211
Tel 1-800/361-1055, 703/361-7300, or Fax 703/335-9486
Quick and easy online ordering: *www.impactpublications.com*

Qty.	Titles	Price	Total

BUSINESS ESSENTIALS

Qty.	Titles	Price	Total
_____	101 Mistakes Employers Make and How to Avoid Them	14.95	_____
_____	101 Secrets of Highly Effective Speakers	14.95	_____
_____	The Best 100 Web Sites for HR Professionals	12.95	_____
_____	Dressing Smart in the New Millennium	13.95	_____
_____	Employer's Guide to Recruiting on the Internet	24.95	_____
_____	Recruit and Retain the Best	14.95	_____
_____	Take This Job and Thrive	14.95	_____

INTERNET JOB SEARCH/HIRING

Qty.	Titles	Price	Total
_____	Career Exploration On the Internet	15.95	_____
_____	Electronic Resumes	19.95	_____
_____	Employer's Guide to Recruiting on the Internet	24.95	_____
_____	Guide to Internet Job Search.	14.95	_____
_____	Heart & Soul Internet Job Search	16.95	_____
_____	How to Get Your Dream Job Using the Web	29.99	_____
_____	Internet Jobs Kit	149.95	_____
_____	Internet Resumes	14.95	_____
_____	Job Searching Online for Dummies	24.99	_____
_____	Resumes in Cyberspace	14.95	_____

ALTERNATIVE JOBS & EMPLOYERS

Qty.	Titles	Price	Total
_____	100 Best Careers for the 21st Century	15.95	_____
_____	100 Great Jobs and How To Get Them	17.95	_____
_____	101 Careers	16.95	_____
_____	150 Best Companies for Liberal Arts Graduates	15.95	_____
_____	50 Coolest Jobs in Sports	15.95	_____
_____	Adams Job Almanac 2000	16.95	_____
_____	American Almanac of Jobs and Salaries	20.00	_____
_____	Back Door Guide to Short-Term Job Adventures	19.95	_____
_____	Best Jobs for the 21st Century	19.95	_____
_____	Breaking & Entering	17.95	_____
_____	Careers in Computers	17.95	_____
_____	Careers in Health Care	17.95	_____
_____	Careers in High Tech	17.95	_____
_____	Career Smarts	12.95	_____

_____	Cool Careers for Dummies	16.95 _____
_____	Cybercareers	24.95 _____
_____	Directory of Executive Recruiters	44.95 _____
_____	Flight Attendant Job Finder	16.95 _____
_____	Great Jobs Ahead	11.95 _____
_____	Health Care Job Explosion!	17.95 _____
_____	Hidden Job Market 2000	18.95 _____
_____	High-Skill, High-Wage Jobs	19.95 _____
_____	JobBank Guide to Computer and High-Tech Companies	16.95 _____
_____	JobSmarts Guide to Top 50 Jobs	15.00 _____
_____	Liberal Arts Jobs	14.95 _____
_____	Media Companies 2000	18.95 _____
_____	Quantum Companies II	26.95 _____
_____	Sunshine Jobs	16.95 _____
_____	Take It From Me	12.00 _____
_____	Top 100	19.95 _____
_____	Top 2,500 Employers 2000	18.95 _____
_____	Trends 2000	14.99 _____
_____	What Employers Really Want	14.95 _____
_____	Working in TV News	12.95 _____
_____	Workstyles to Fit Your Lifestyle	11.95 _____
_____	You Can't Play the Game If You Don't Know the Rules	14.95 _____

RECRUITERS/EMPLOYERS

_____	Adams Executive Recruiters Almanac	16.95 _____
_____	Directory of Executive Recruiters	44.95 _____
_____	Employer's Guide to Recruiting on the Internet	24.95 _____

JOB STRATEGIES AND TACTICS

_____	101 Ways to Power Up Your Job Search	12.95 _____
_____	110 Big Mistakes Job Hunters	19.95 _____
_____	24 Hours to Your Next Job, Raise, or Promotion	10.95 _____
_____	Better Book for Getting Hired	11.95 _____
_____	Career Bounce-Back	14.95 _____
_____	Career Chase	17.95 _____
_____	Career Fitness	19.95 _____
_____	Career Intelligence	15.95 _____
_____	Career Starter	10.95 _____
_____	Coming Alive From 9 to 5	18.95 _____
_____	Complete Idiot's Guide to Changing Careers	17.95 _____
_____	Executive Job Search Strategies	16.95 _____
_____	First Job Hunt Survival Guide	11.95 _____
_____	Five Secrets to Finding a Job	12.95 _____
_____	Get a Job You Love!	19.95 _____
_____	Get It Together By 30	14.95 _____
_____	Get the Job You Want Series	37.95 _____
_____	Get Ahead! Stay Ahead!	12.95 _____
_____	Getting from Fired to Hired	14.95 _____
_____	Great Jobs for Liberal Arts Majors	11.95 _____
_____	How to Get a Job in 90 Days or Less	12.95 _____
_____	How to Get Interviews from Classified Job Ads	14.95 _____
_____	How to Succeed Without a Career Path	13.95 _____
_____	How to Get the Job You Really Want	9.95 _____
_____	How to Make Use of a Useless Degree	13.00 _____
_____	Is It Too Late To Run Away and Join the Circus?	14.95 _____
_____	Job Hunting in the 21st Century	17.95 _____
_____	Job Hunting for the Utterly Confused	14.95 _____
_____	Job Hunting Made Easy	12.95 _____
_____	Job Search: The Total System	14.95 _____
_____	Job Search Organizer	12.95 _____
_____	Job Search Time Manager	14.95 _____
_____	JobShift	13.00 _____
_____	JobSmart	12.00 _____

146 Take This Job and Thrive

_____	Kiplinger's Survive and Profit From a Mid-Career Change	12.95 _____
_____	Knock 'Em Dead	12.95 _____
_____	Me, Myself, and I, Inc.	17.95 _____
_____	New Rights of Passage	29.95 _____
_____	No One Is Unemployable	29.95 _____
_____	Not Just Another Job	12.00 _____
_____	Part-Time Careers	10.95 _____
_____	Perfect Job Search	12.95 _____
_____	Princeton Review Guide to Your Career	20.00 _____
_____	Perfect Pitch	13.99 _____
_____	Portable Executive	12.00 _____
_____	Professional's Job Finder	18.95 _____
_____	Reinventing Your Career	9.99 _____
_____	Resumes Don't Get Jobs	10.95 _____
_____	Right Fit	14.95 _____
_____	Right Place at the Right Time	11.95 _____
_____	Second Careers	14.95 _____
_____	Secrets from the Search Firm Files	24.95 _____
_____	So What If I'm 50	12.95 _____
_____	Staying in Demand	12.95 _____
_____	Strategic Job Jumping	13.00 _____
_____	SuccessAbilities	14.95 _____
_____	Take Yourself to the Top	13.99 _____
_____	Temping: The Insiders Guide	14.95 _____
_____	Top 10 Career Strategies for the Year 2000 & Beyond	12.00 _____
_____	Top 10 Fears of Job Seekers	12.00 _____
_____	Ultimate Job Search Survival	14.95 _____
_____	VGMs Career Checklist	9.95 _____
_____	Welcome to the Real World	13.00 _____
_____	What Do I Say Next?	20.00 _____
_____	What Employers Really Want	14.95 _____
_____	When Do I Start	11.95 _____
_____	Who Says There Are No Jobs Out There	12.95 _____
_____	Work Happy Live Healthy	14.95 _____
_____	Work This Way	14.95 _____

ATTITUDE & MOTIVATION

_____	100 Ways to Motivate Yourself	15.99 _____
_____	Attitude Is Everything	14.99 _____
_____	Change Your Attitude	15.99 _____
_____	Reinventing Yourself	18.99 _____

INSPIRATION & EMPOWERMENT

_____	10 Stupid Things Men Do to Mess Up Their Lives	13.00 _____
_____	10 Stupid Things Women Do	13.00 _____
_____	101 Great Resumes	9.99 _____
_____	101 Simple Ways to Be Good to Yourself	12.95 _____
_____	Awaken the Giant Within	12.00 _____
_____	Beating Job Burnout	12.95 _____
_____	Big Things Happen When You Do the Little Things Right	15.00 _____
_____	Career Busters	10.95 _____
_____	Chicken Soup for the Soul Series	87.95 _____
_____	Do What You Love, the Money Will Follow	11.95 _____
_____	Doing It All Isn't Everything	19.95 _____
_____	Doing Work You Love	14.95 _____
_____	Emotional Intelligence	13.95 _____
_____	First Things First	23.00 _____
_____	Get What You Deserve	23.00 _____
_____	Getting Unstuck	11.99 _____
_____	If It's Going To Be, It's Up To Me	22.00 _____
_____	If Life Is A Game, These Are the Rules	15.00 _____
_____	In Search of Values	8.99 _____
_____	Job/Family Challenge: A 9-5 Guide	12.95 _____

_____	Kick In the Seat of the Pants	11.95 _____
_____	Kiplinger's Taming the Paper Tiger	11.95 _____
_____	Life Skills	17.95 _____
_____	Love Your Work and SuccessWill Follow	12.95 _____
_____	Path, The	14.95 _____
_____	Personal Job Power	12.95 _____
_____	Power of Purpose	20.00 _____
_____	Seven Habits of Highly Effective People	14.00 _____
_____	Softpower	10.95 _____
_____	Stop Postponing the Rest of Your Life	9.95 _____
_____	Suvivor Personality	12.00 _____
_____	To Build the Life You Want, Create the Work You Love	10.95 _____
_____	Unlimited Power	12.00 _____
_____	Wake-Up Calls	18.95 _____
_____	Your Signature Path	24.95 _____

TESTING AND ASSESSMENT

_____	Career Counselor's Tool Kit	45.00 _____
_____	Career Discovery Project	12.95 _____
_____	Career Exploration Inventory	29.95 _____
_____	Career Satisfaction and Success	14.95 _____
_____	Career Tests	12.95 _____
_____	Crystal-Barkley Guideto Taking Charge of Your Career	9.95 _____
_____	Dictionary of Holland Occupational Codes	45.00 _____
_____	Discover the Best Jobs For You	14.95 _____
_____	Discover What You're Best At	12.00 _____
_____	Gifts Differing	14.95 _____
_____	Have You Got What It Takes?	12.95 _____
_____	How to Find the Work You Love	10.95 _____
_____	Making Vocational Choices	29.95 _____
_____	New Quick Job Hunting Map	4.95 _____
_____	P.I.E. Method for Career Success	14.95 _____
_____	Putting Your Talent to Work	12.95 _____
_____	Real People, Real Jobs	15.95 _____
_____	Starting Out, Starting Over	14.95 _____
_____	Test Your IQ	6.95 _____
_____	Three Boxes of Life	18.95 _____
_____	Type Talk	11.95 _____
_____	WORKTypes	12.99 _____
_____	You and Co., Inc.	22.00 _____
_____	Your Hidden Assets	19.95 _____

RESUMES & LETTERS

_____	$110,000 Resume	16.95 _____
_____	100 Winning Resumes for $100,000+ Jobs	24.95 _____
_____	101 Best Resumes	10.95 _____
_____	101 More Best Resumes	11.95 _____
_____	101 Quick Tips for a Dynamite Resume	13.95 _____
_____	1500+ Key Words for 100,000+	14.95 _____
_____	175 High-Impact Resumes	10.95 _____
_____	Adams Resume Almanac/Disk	19.95 _____
_____	America's Top Resumes for America's Top Jobs	19.95 _____
_____	Asher's Bible of Exec.utive Resumes	29.95 _____
_____	Best Resumes for $75,000+ Executive Jobs	14.95 _____
_____	Best Resumes for Attorneys	16.95 _____
_____	Better Resumes in Three Easy Steps	12.95 _____
_____	Blue Collar and Beyond	8.95 _____
_____	Blue Collar Resumes	11.99 _____
_____	Building a Great Resume	15.00 _____
_____	Complete Idiot's Guide to Writing the Perfect Resume	16.95 _____
_____	Conquer Resume Objections	10.95 _____
_____	Creating Your High School Resume and Portfolio	13.90 _____
_____	Creating Your Skills Portfolio	10.95 _____

	Cyberspace Resume Kit	16.95	
	Damn Good Resume Guide	7.95	
	Dynamite Resumes	14.95	
	Edge Resume and Job Search Strategy	23.95	
	Electronic Resumes and Onlline Networking	13.99	
	Encyclopedia of Job-Winning Resumes	16.95	
	Gallery of Best Resumes	16.95	
	Heart & Soul Resumes	15.95	
	High Impact Resumes and Letters	19.95	
	Just Resumes	11.95	
	New Perfect Resume	10.95	
	Overnight Resume	12.95	
	Portfolio Power	14.95	
	Power Resumes	14.95	
	Prof. Resumes/Executives, Managers, & Other Administrators	19.95	
	Professional "Resumes For..." Career Series	213.95	
	Quick Resume and Cover Letter Book	12.95	
	Ready-To-Go Resumes	29.95	
	Resume Catalog	15.95	
	Resume Magic	18.95	
	Resume Power	12.95	
	Resume Pro	24.95	
	Resume Shortcuts	14.95	
	Resume Writing Made Easy	11.95	
	Resumes for the Over-50 Job Hunter	14.95	
	Resumes for Re-Entry	10.95	
	Resume Winners from the Pros	17.95	
	Resumes for Dummies	12.99	
	Resumes for the Health Care Professional	14.95	
	Resumes That Knock 'Em Dead	10.95	
	Resumes That Will Get You the Job You Want	12.99	
	Savvy Resume Writer	10.95	
	Sure-Hire Resumes	14.95	
	Winning Resumes	10.95	

COVER LETTERS

	101 Best Cover Letters	11.95	
	175 High-Impact Cover Letters	10.95	
	200 Letters for Job Hunters	19.95	
	201 Winning Cover Letters for the $100,000+ Jobs	24.95	
	201 Dynamite Job Search Letters	19.95	
	201 Killer Cover Letters	16.95	
	Complete Idiot's Guide to the Perfect Cover Letters	14.95	
	Cover Letters for Dummies	12.99	
	Cover Letters that Knock 'Em Dead	10.95	
	Dynamite Cover Letters	14.95	
	Gallery of Best Cover Letters	18.95	
	Haldane's Best Cover Letters for Professionals	15.95	
	Perfect Cover Letter	10.95	
	Winning Cover Letters	10.95	

ETIQUETTE AND IMAGE

	Business Etiquette and Professionalism	10.95	
	Dressing Smart in the New Millennium	13.95	
	Executive Etiquette in the New Workplace	14.95	
	First Five Minutes	14.95	
	John Malloy's Dress for Success (For Men)	13.99	
	Lions Don't Need to Roar	10.99	
	New Professional Image	12.95	
	New Women's Dress for Success	12.99	
	Red Socks Don't Work	14.95	
	Winning Image	17.95	
	You've Only Got 3 Seconds	22.95	

INTERVIEWING: JOBSEEKERS

_____	101 Dynamite Answers to Interview Questions	12.95 _____
_____	101 Dynamite Questions to Ask at Your Job Interview	14.95 _____
_____	101 Tough Interview Questions. . .	14.95 _____
_____	111 Dynamite Ways to Ace Your Job Interview	13.95 _____
_____	Haldane's Best Answers to Tough Interview Questions	15.95 _____
_____	Information Interviewing	10.95 _____
_____	Interview for Success	15.95 _____
_____	Job Interviews for Dummies	12.99 _____
_____	Savvy Interviewer	10.95 _____

NETWORKING

_____	Dig Your Well Before You're Thirsty	24.95 _____
_____	Dynamite Networking for Dynamite Jobs	15.95 _____
_____	Dynamite Tele-Search	12.95 _____
_____	Golden Rule of Schmoozing	12.95 _____
_____	Great Connections	11.95 _____
_____	How to Work a Room	11.99 _____
_____	Network Your Way to Success	19.95 _____
_____	Networking for Everyone	16.95 _____
_____	Power Networking	14.95 _____
_____	Power Schmoozing	12.95 _____
_____	Power To Get In	24.95 _____

SALARY NEGOTIATIONS

_____	Dynamite Salary Negotiations	15.95 _____
_____	Get a Raise in 7 Days	14.95 _____
_____	Get More Money on Your Next Job	14.95 _____
_____	Negotiate Your Job Offer	14.95 _____

☞ **SUBTOTAL** $ _____

☞ Virginia residents add 4½% sales tax) _____

☞ Shipping/handling, Continental U.S., $5.00 + $5.00
plus following percentages when **SUBTOTAL** is:

   ❑ $30-$100—multiply SUBTOTAL by 8% _____

   ❑ $100-$999—multiply SUBTOTAL by 7% _____

   ❑ $1,000-$4,999—multiply SUBTOTAL by 6% _____

   ❑ Over $5,000—multiply SUBTOTAL by 5% _____

☞   ❑ If shipped outside Continental US, add another 5% _____

☞ **TOTAL ENCLOSED** $ _____

SHIP TO: (street address only for UPS or RPS delivery)

Name _____

Address _____

_____

_____

Telephone _____

I enclose ❑ Check ❑ Money Order in the amount of: $ _____

Charge $_____ to ❑ Visa ❑ MC ❑ AmEx

Card # _____ Exp: _____ / _____

Signature _____

Discover Hundreds of Additional Resources on the World Wide Web!

Looking for the newest and best books, directories, newsletters, wall charts, training programs, videos, computer software, and kits to help you land a job, negotiate a higher salary, or start your own business? Want to learn the most effective way to find a job in Asia or relocate to San Francisco? Are you curious about how to find a job 24 hours a day using the Internet or about what you'll be doing five years from now? Are you trying to keep up-to-date on the latest career resources, but are not able to find the latest catalogs, brochures, or newsletters on today's "best of the best" resources?

Welcome to the first virtual career bookstore on the Internet. Now you're only a click away with Impact Publications' electronic solution to the resource challenge. Visit this rich site to quickly discover everything you ever wanted to know about finding jobs, changing careers, and starting your own business—including many useful resources that are difficult to find in local bookstores and libraries. The site also includes what's new and hot, tips for job search success, and monthly specials. Check it out today!

www.impactpublications.com